DARYL TRAVIS
— with Harrison Yates —

LITTLE
THINGS
BIG RETURNS

HOW TO DELIVER EXPERIENCES THAT
MATTER MOST TO YOUR CUSTOMERS

*I*t has long been an axiom of mine that the little things are infinitely the most important.

~ *Arthur Conan Doyle*

DARYL TRAVIS

— with Harrison Yates —

LITTLE
THINGS
BIG RETURNS

HOW TO DELIVER EXPERIENCES THAT MATTER MOST TO YOUR CUSTOMERS

THE BIG PICTURE

CHAPTER 1

Right from the Start

A FRIEND OF MINE ONCE TOLD ME A WONDERFUL STORY ABOUT the time he took his grandfather's watch to a jeweler to get it running years after it had stopped. It was a watch his grandfather had worn all the way through combat in World War II, and it had great sentimental value far beyond its monetary worth. When he went to pick up the watch, the jeweler surprised him by saying there would be no charge—he fixed the watch in gratitude for the grandfather's service in the military.

You can bet my friend will never go to another jeweler as long as he lives, and he will tell and retell this story over and over again, thus creating new potential customers for this very thoughtful jeweler.

Most people have a story of a great customer experience they easily recall and are more than happy to share. My favorite is the time the water pump went out in my new Audi Q5. This happened during the introduction of my specific model and Audi had only just discovered the problem, creating a long delay in getting a replacement pump. Audi provided me with a loaner vehicle so I wasn't terribly inconvenienced, but after a nearly two-week delay, the situation was getting irksome. I was about to become a difficult, complaining customer when Audi's corporate office took the initiative, seized the moment and called me to say, "We're sorry. We know this is not right and we'd like to try to make it up to you. So, we're going to give you an extended service agreement and warranty for the life of the lease on your car. During the remaining term of your lease, all service charges are on us."

Well that was it for me. I was an Audi fan and now, thanks to that experience, I am a devoted Audi fan, if not a brand zealot. I'm delighted to share the story whenever I have the chance, and I am fairly sure I've sold about a dozen Audis to my friends. I also love to use it as an example of the challenge of every brand and every marketer—to create an authentic brand experience that inspires customer trust and loyalty. Unfortunately, like most people, I also have stories of the most awful customer experiences you can imagine. Just wait until you read the next chapter.

This book shows you how highly successful companies hone in on critical moments in the experience of their brands to create long-lasting loyalties. It shows how there may be dozens or even hundreds of touchpoints along the customer's journey with your brand, but only a few create the emotionally resonant moments that draw us in or turn us away. Brands that discover those moments are able to focus their time and resources on what matters most to customers and the experiences that truly engender loyalty.

A good way to understand what I mean is to think about those moments that become the stories people tell about you, and how the most emotionally meaningful ones become the defining elements of your brand. When they are favorable, they become experiential sweet spots your customers come to depend on and may even fall in love with.

The starting point often originates in one divinely simple idea: The little things you do matter a great deal more than the big things you say. By "little things," I mean the right things, the decent human things— kindnesses and considerations that make an indelible impression that people never forget.

Two things are revealed in the stories in this book: one, a meaningful experience is a small kindness that feels like a decent, authentic human gesture of good will; and two, it often takes a customer by surprise, creating a unique and memorable experience aside from any other expectation, including product quality, a fair price, a pleasant store or any other touchpoint. By its very nature, doing the right thing cannot be manufactured. It can only occur one customer at a time, which is why it comes down to establishing a company-wide culture of trusting and caring that begins not with customers, but with how well you care for your employees. It is the simple truth that you can't just write into a formal business or marketing plan. It is the real life experience of truth and trust that builds and binds internal *and* external loyalty at the same time.

TRUTH AND TRUST

Trust is essential because it makes it possible to know who and what we can depend on. For all the goodness trust provides, it's also quite risky because we put ourselves at the mercy of whatever we deem to be trustworthy. More than anything else, the role of a brand is to create trust. Customers want and need brands to live up to what they promise. But, tellingly, we are not surprised when brands disappoint. Instead, as in my experience with Audi, we are amazed and delighted when brands don't let us down.

When anything is as crucial as trust, we should understand exactly what it is and how is it earned. David DeSteno explores a substantial body of research on the subject in his book *The Truth About Trust.* His review of the science concludes that the most essential mental processes of the human mind are wired to habitually seek fairness. We constantly scan and automatically screen for betrayal and mistrust because the need to trust others is critical to our survival. So much so that behavioral economists have demonstrated in numerous experiments and studies that people will reject unfair offers that violate their sense of trust, even if it costs them something to do so.

We judge fairness and come to trust friends as a result of our interactions with them. It feels good when a friend says, "I'm here for you," but it's only when she is there for us reliably that she earns our trust. It's only then that we truly trust she is able to meet our needs and will always do so. Human minds process brands in a similar way. Three experiential elements become the criteria for a brand's trustworthiness:

1. What is the brand's purpose or promise—is it something wanted and needed?
2. Is the brand competent and capable of delivering what it promises?
3. Does the brand consistently demonstrate integrity and conviction to do what it promises?

Executives, chief marketing officers and brand managers all share an obligation to make sure their brands can be trusted in everything they *say and do*. We need to realize a brand becomes trusted more by the things it does, the experience it provides, rather than the things it says. Every marketer needs to take responsibility for engendering trust throughout the whole brand experience and assume accountability for how much his or her brand can be trusted.

Most marketing people will contend, of course, that they are working to build trust in their brands. Yet, Sean Moffitt and Mike Dover point out in their book, *Wikibrands*, that only 8 percent of people trust what companies say, and only 17 percent believe companies take their customers seriously. Study after study suggests people only trust brands that their friends recommend, which really means they trust their friends, not the brands.

A company's reputation and sense of purpose provide revealing insights into whether or not customers can trust the company. When companies have a higher purpose beyond just making money, we start to think they are trustworthy. Once they demonstrate integrity—actually doing the right thing—we believe they are truly trustworthy. But trust this—if it's not true, your customers will know. Promises made and kept must be authentic. These attributes cannot be faked, and customer expectations will not be met with lip service. That's why creating and delivering a trustable brand experience becomes the imperative for every marketer, and the results for which every business professional should be accountable.

HIGH RETURN ON TRUST

In a CNBC interview from the World Economic Conference in Davos, Richard Branson commended CEO Paul Polman for transforming the "whole of Unilever into a force for good." Branson also claimed "the shareholders seem to be doing okay with it." Unilever is not alone in the quest for a higher purpose. None other than Walmart has embraced an enlightened purpose to improve the company's social and environmental impact.

When we see such passion from the likes of Unilever and Walmart, it won't be long before they pass their commitment along to their suppliers and channel partners. Branson also mentioned Polman is "getting suppliers to become a force for good, buying right, where they're buying from and not cutting down the rain forest." Anyone who sells to Walmart has experienced the ripple effect of the company's demands. If you do business with these or any of the growing number of other purpose-driven consumer giants, expect to become not only partners in business but also partners in purpose. When companies sincerely demonstrate a higher purpose, quest, mission, ideals or whatever we call it—it's that much easier to trust them.

Companies do not embrace higher order motives because it's bad for business. The fact is for-profit companies that pursue and internalize a heroic cause for their brands are highly profitable. It appears that doing good and doing well can indeed be part and parcel of the objective of growth and higher profit, and more companies see the financial and psychological advantages of pursing a higher calling. Leading by and with purpose is a philosophical and practical imperative. Trust creates loyalty. Loyalty builds profits. Profits make the mission possible. As I remind my one and only socialist-leaning friend, "No margin, no mission."

The practical, competitive power of purpose is also increasingly embraced by business-to-business enterprises. IBM's "Let's make a smarter planet" is the expression of its calling to improve education and health care. Dow Chemical leverages its tradition of innovation to make canola and sunflower seeds that produce oils with lower levels of saturated fat and no trans fats. Becton Dickenson developed the world's first syringe to protect health workers from needle-stick injuries that can cause HIV and other infections. This purposeful initiative turned into a $2 billion dollar business that accounts for 25 percent of the company's revenue.

If you're faced with finding purpose for your organization, don't despair. There is always more to what you do than just banging out the quarterly numbers. Don't think about what you do or how you do it; instead, consider *why* you do it. What is the real value in the mind of your customer? What would she say you do to improve her life, and how would she describe it? What is better in the world because of what you do?

Focused purpose is like courage—it doesn't work in half measure. A CEO can only expect to inspire employees once he or she provides a clear and simple articulation of why the company exists. A higher order ideal establishes emotional appeal and stirs trust among all of your stakeholders to, even in a small way, be a part of the company's quest. Then, and only then, will employees and customers know why they should care and what they should do.

The idea is not to create departmental silos for the different functions within your organization. The suggestion is that your staff, customers, suppliers, investors, along with internal and external communications, deserve to be served from one big pot of heart-warming stew of authentic intent, and that intent becomes more appealing when it is tied to a higher cause. This is when your brand becomes the trusted one simply because, to the outside world, your employees *are* the brand and they perform best when they work for meaning as well as money.

Everybody in the company must be given the authority to be his or her own trust department because the folks you sell to make no distinction between your product or service and the people who make and represent it. It's all one and the same, and you will find this to be true in your own experience, as in when you go to a department store and can't find anyone to help you. Or if you are having trouble with your phone and get an infuriating recorded message from your provider rather than a helpful person to clear up the trouble in person. When things go wrong, you blame the people at the store or the phone company or the airline counter just as much as the product itself. When the opposite happens (and it thankfully does), you credit the brand because the brand and the people who represent it are inseparable.

Your purpose becomes the focus of everything, the beacon that keeps your company from veering into tempting distractions. It guides strategy, communications, customer service, employee engagement, change management, innovation, operations, everything. It provides the benchmark, the audit of how well you are doing and how much you can be trusted. Ultimately, a greater degree of trustworthiness contributes to a materially improved, broad-based perception in terms of what people feel about the intrinsic value of your company.

A LOW COST ATTITUDE ADJUSTMENT

How much does it cost to have empathy for your customers? Actually, not much—in fact, it's virtually free. All it costs is a change in your attitude. You merely have to put your customer's needs and desires at the center of everything you do in place of your company's internal-facing, self-serving motives. Every company invests in product development, sales and customer service. Time and money are routinely devoted to strategic plans and budgets, operating procedures and training programs devised for employees to make it all happen. When those same resources are refocused on truly understanding and meeting customer needs instead of internal operations is when you realize that, more than anything, customers appreciate being treated the same way you want to be treated. Human kindness, dignity, decency and respect are little things—right things—that take you a long, long way toward winning delighted, loyal customers. Doing the right thing just because it is the right thing pays incredible dividends. It is quite liberating to realize there are many little, inexpensive things that earn big returns, and to realize that it is not necessary to redo your whole business, turn it upside-down or turn it inside out to win customers' hearts and minds.

Although it is not costly to change your attitude, you will need to be very thoughtful in how to go about it because you simply cannot leave out the human touch. Research confirms why your intentions must be authentic and that you will not change your attitude by analyzing the situation and coldly calculating a strategy to empathize with employees and customers. It doesn't work because Dr. Anthony Jack and other researchers have discovered when your brain is engaged in cold hard analysis, it automatically suppresses the network of neurons used for empathy. Our brains are just not wired to make connections between our social, emotional and moral motivations and the network of neurons we use for scientific, mathematical and logical reasoning. "You want the CEO of a company to be highly analytical in order to run a company efficiently, otherwise it will go out of business. But, you can lose your moral compass if you get stuck in an analytic way of thinking. You'll never get by without both networks. You don't want to favor one, but cycle efficiently between them, and employ the right network at the right time" says Dr. Jack in the journal *Neuroimage*.

If your business mind struggles to overcome its self-serving biases, an even better question may be, "How much does it cost if you don't change your attitude?" You will find a compelling argument for customer empathy as you read in the next chapter what happens to a company when its cold hard business nature takes over and costs it everything.

Fortunately, as you will discover in the remaining chapters of this book, when you're passionate about doing the right things for the right reasons, your customers trust you and beat a well-worn path to your door. Your business thrives and becomes an exciting, flourishing, healthy, vital part of public life and even plays a role in making this crazy world just a little bit better every day.

Should you need any more encouragement, it's good to remember Mark Twain's advice: "Always do right. This will gratify some people and astonish the rest."

CHAPTER 2

Truth or Consequences

IT WAS JUST TWENTY-FIVE YEARS AGO ON THE EXACT DAY I AM writing this when an Oxford University physicist by the name of Tim Berners Lee invented the World Wide Web. I wonder if he and his academic colleagues knew the extent to which they were profoundly changing the way we work, play and live our lives.

Our need to connect and communicate with each other in large part explains the phenomenon of the web. We are, after all, still driven by the same basic social and survival instincts that have always motivated human beings. It's easy to exaggerate the effects of the web, but when a kid in preschool can hold a device in one hand that puts her in touch with all the knowledge in the world, you have to gasp at what this means for the future of that world. And since there are now more of these devices in circulation than there are people, the ability to find, share and challenge knowledge becomes all the more mind-boggling. It all has vast social consequences that go well beyond the scope of this book, but how some of those consequences affect the ways we conduct our basic business lives and how we will treat our customers are profound.

Companies used to believe they could decide what their customers needed to know and spoon fed that information to them by spending large amounts of money on relentlessly repetitive advertising. Some advertising agencies did this very well for their clients, and the people doing the most involving work were in some circles considered creative geniuses. As we will see in this book, those days are gone forever and no one mourns the loss because those practices are being replaced by something far better—authentic, meaningful customer experiences.

It's not that media advertising doesn't work, though it doesn't influence as much as it once did. In his book *Tribes*, Seth Godin reminds us, "People don't believe what you tell them. They rarely believe what you show them. They believe what their friends tell them." It's that the ability to communicate one-on-one is expanding the repertoire of persuasions and it's natural for us to prefer person-to-person exchanges because we have reason to trust them more.

Although not as ominous as it sometimes sounds, companies increasingly have access to where we are and what we are thinking and doing at any given moment. We can see this as a threat to our privacy or as an opportunity for brands to be more connected to and meet our needs even better. A colorful example of this comes from the Cinnamon Toasty Crunch cereal brand, which picked up on millennial males' back-and-forth social media conversations about how they snack on the stuff at night. Typically, the target audience for the brand has always been mothers feeding it to their little ones, but some bright marketer got the idea of creating social media messages aimed at young males with cheeky comments like "Good in bed" and "Spoon with me." It's fun and shows the company understands quite well at least one group of its customers through their real experiences with the brand. It makes the advertising become a more relevant experience because it connects with customers on their real world level. The brand might also demonstrate even more how they truly appreciate the customer's experience by working a deal with Netflix to offer customers reduced late-night rates to games and movies. We might say the old adage "a picture is worth a thousand words" has become "one great experience is worth a thousand ads."

A supermarket can now talk to you the minute you go into the store with a beep on your smart phone and a message alerting you to a sale on canned salmon in aisle fourteen. The technology now exists to hook your car up so that when your windshield wipers get a bit worn, you can get advanced warning. A message also might appear on your car computer telling you about a nearby garage that just happens to have a special on wipers this very day. You can use your smart phone to arm your home security system, turn the lights on and off, start the coffee and feed the cat. Smarter and easier-to-use technologies monitor and track sleep, exercise, calories and all of your body's physiological vitals, and make suggestions on how you can improve your health. It all sounds downright Orwellian, but it is not yet Big Brother watching you. It is companies looking for meaningful ways to become a useful part of your everyday experience, and with The Internet of Things, where everything in your life, including your own body, is hooked up to a device that is always with you, it will only become more so. I look forward, with some chagrin, to the day when my fridge and pantry are stocked with foods my watch ordered for delivery because it knows before I do that I've gained a few pounds and my blood pressure is up several points.

What it all means is that the Internet is making the business of business more personal than it has ever been. When I was in the advertising agency business, I used to say we may indeed buy media based on cost-per-thousand, but effective communication is always based on cost-per-one. I was part of the then-new school that saw people as individuals rather than as demographic objects, as so many advertisers did in more Jurassic days. I hated designations like DINKS (double-income-no kids), BOBOS (bourgeois bohemians) and other inanities that bear no resemblance beyond the extreme surface of what makes people who and what they are. They were all the rage a few years ago to accommodate a mass market view of the world, but the ability to engage people with one-on-one dialogue has obviously made a huge difference in how brands can be in touch and stay in touch with individuals (and vice versa) rather than some superficial marketing jabber.

CUSTOMER AS FRIEND AND PARTNER

I think it was Victorian merchants who coined the phrase, "The customer knows best." It survives to this day, but I never liked it because to me it suggests obvious pandering rather than looking out for the customer's welfare and enjoyment of an experience. And sometimes a customer can be very wrong, as when he or she insults or mistreats one of your employees and should be summarily corrected as politely as your temper makes possible!

Customers and businesses can now work together as never before to achieve not just satisfaction, but personal and mutual appreciation. As social beings, our survival depends on the need to be accepted and approved by our families, friends and others we interact with routinely. Personal approval establishes a benchmark for how *all* of our other interactions are interpreted and evaluated in our minds. This need is at the heart of the concept of reciprocity—you scratch my back and I'll scratch yours. In the same manner, a brand that makes you feel accepted will win your acceptance, if not your undying loyalty.

The power and inherent social need for reciprocity explains, in large part, why customer service is fast giving way to an emphasis on customer experience. The brands featured in this book provide good examples. As already noted, when you achieve successful customer collaboration on the delivery of an outstanding experience, you also create enthusiastic word-of-mouth advocates. In effect, your customers become your marketing department, and this is made possible with agile use of one-on-one experiences that provoke reciprocity.

DEMOCRACY RULES

Winston Churchill once said, "Democracy is the worst form of government, except for all the others that have been tried from time to time." Some people in business might agree when they see that the digital age has wrought unprecedented business transparency. Your customers know where you live, and woe unto the companies who think they can get away with anything other than authentic concern for their customer's welfare. We now live in a global village where democracy rules. The peasant can have as much say as the king. As said in an IBM C-Suite Survey, "The emergence of social, mobile and digital networks has played a big part in democratizing the relationship between organizations and their customers. It is forcing them to rethink how they work." Business is being forced to develop a keener conscience based on a newfound awareness of the greater good.

These are all topics we might never have discussed even fifteen years ago. There were a few visionaries around like Peter Drucker as far back as the 1950s who showed the way, but they were by far the exception. It is mainly today's young entrepreneurs who totally get it. Growing up digitally savvy, they are the new pioneers who understand the concepts that start with quests involving stories of experiences and social responsibilities as the way to conduct successful, profitable, fulfilling commerce. Some, like Marc Zuckerberg and Elon Musk, actually see themselves changing the world. Even many huge multinationals now see the value of investing in caring for customer sensibilities beyond the utility of their offerings. And, of course, being an employee in these kinds of companies has never been more rewarding as managers come to the awareness that the employee *is* the brand and *must* have an emotional stake in its fortunes and mutual success. The Zuckerbergs and Musks of the new business landscape totally grasp the idea that business is about service and that it works best when service extends to society at large, not just within a brand's practical promise.

POWER TO THE PEOPLE

I read recently that 40 percent of baby boomers believe most people can be trusted, but only 19 percent of millennials share that view. Ironically, it seems the most connected generation in human history has experienced the least amount of social trust.

This troublesome reality profoundly touches your brand and how people out there feel about it, and perhaps it is the dearth of trust that might partly explain why so many young people nowadays gravitate to non-profit companies in the quest for personal fulfillment rather than go the corporate route. It also does not help that many of them are up to their eyeballs in debt from the cost of their educations and cannot find satisfying work in their chosen fields. But I'm convinced the transparency possible through closer connections and better experiences could rescue them from wholesale cynicism. Injustices both big and small can now be aired and shared at lightning speed. One of my favorite examples comes from the Makers Mark bourbon brand. The brand decided they could broaden the appeal of its taste by watering it down to make it a little less strong. The decision sent the brand's customer devotees into a literal fervor of protest, which forced a return to the old formula. A well-loved brand of orange juice got into trouble when it changed its packaging. The old package had imagery of a straw sticking out of an orange that had become an iconic beacon of experience and trust to the customer. The new one got rid of the straw and started a customer rebellion—the brand lost nearly 30 percent of its business in just a few weeks! When people can do this with individual products, think about what it means for brands, companies and even governments they feel are betraying their trust. Just ask the government officials overthrown in what has become known as the Arab Spring. Executives and politicians alike had better listen up!

This book celebrates the positive rather than the finger-wagging negative, but I find it useful to start with a dramatic example of a personal horror show that had a profound effect on my thinking about how *not* to run a business. I thought if I shared what a bad brand does wrong, we could get a clearer picture of how a good brand might do it right.

CHAPTER 3

How to Lose Friends and Make
People Hate You

THE EVENT GOES BACK TO THE YEAR 2000. THE FACT THAT IT lingers in my memory and can still get my blood boiling when I think about it tells you how deeply a negative customer experience can get stamped into people's hearts and minds.

I was in Detroit after a good day with a client and eager to get on a flight home to Chicago. The airline necessitated by my schedule was Northwest. Traveling often, I try not get too fussed about minor delays and inconveniences. The minute I start packing my bag, I have learned to go into a sort of self-preservation Zen mode that helps me deal with the standard annoyances of air travel. The experience of that long-ago flight has proved to be good training for tolerating the routine hassles of getting around now.

SHOW ME THE WAY TO GO HOME.

Arriving at the airport in mid afternoon, I discovered that several Chicago flights had already been cancelled. There was no problem with the weather, so I wondered when the Northwest people would bother themselves to tell the gathering crowd what was wrong. They never did, and in a situation like that, no news is not good news. After every announcement of yet another cancelation, you could hear a collective groan reverberate through the terminal. This was eventually followed by audible sighs of relief when my fellow passengers and I happily got on board the next-to-last flight and the plane taxied to the runway.

The smiles froze, however, as we sat motionless on the ramp for a minor eternity. One hour went by. Then another. After several announcements of mechanical problems from the cabin crew, the pilot eventually announced that the reason for the delay was weather in Chicago. You could not help but wonder how long Northwest people thought this suspicious weather was likely to last.

ONE STEP FORWARD, TWO BACK

It's a horrible, sinking feeling when a plane returns to the gate, which is exactly where we ended up. We were told we would have to go to the main terminal ticket counter to get advice on our alternatives. If you remember Detroit's old airport, you know this was not pleasant news. It was a long, miserable trek to get anywhere in that dismal labyrinth, but I still had my stoic hat on and did my best to go with the flow.

I saw the departure time for the last flight was drawing near – not that it mattered much because I knew that four other cancelled planeloads of angry souls were as anxious as I was to get a seat on that last flight, and the chances might be slim.

After schlepping back to the main counter with lines from here to kingdom come, I actually witnessed a Northwest customer service agent yelling at an elderly lady for asking a simple question. It became more and more obvious that I would not get on the last flight out.

FEAR AND LOATHING IN DETROIT

Finally, I resigned to simply retrieving my bag, staying the night and getting on another carrier in the morning. I say another carrier because I calmly resolved to, at all costs, avoid Northwest, if I possibly could, for the rest of my life. But as the Scottish bard said, the best laid schemes of mice and men often go astray, and this is the point where the real fun began.

The baggage handling crew had left for the day. Left for the day!

Bags from several cancelled flights were simply not available, at all. I had medications and contact lens paraphernalia in my bag that I couldn't get. What's worse is everyone's bags had been tossed into a temporary holding area; I could actually see my bag about twenty feet from where I was standing. I could see it, but I couldn't have it. This was about all the provocation I could take, and suddenly I lost my proverbial cool. At the top of my lungs I demanded my bag "*NOW*, OR I WILL NEVER FLY NORTHWEST *EVER AGAIN*." The passengers around me applauded loudly, and the Northwest agent responded with a glare.

SEE YA LATER, PAL

The airline offered nothing. Not to me. Not to anyone. No advice. No hotel. No transportation. No rebooking confirmation. No apology. And to add insult to injury, no bag, even though it was in plain sight. Nada. In fact, I am convinced the customer service people had taken special training in how to behave like attack dogs because human beings are not naturally that evil to one another. (Come to find out later, union problems spawned the whole traumatic experience.)

I had to rent a car, find a drug store late at night in a city I did not know well, buy the usual necessities, and find a hotel room for which I had to pay double. You might think it couldn't get any worse, but it did.

THE DOUBLE WHAMMY

After I arrived back in Chicago via another carrier the next day, I began the process of finding my bag. For more than six hours, my assistant and I tried to reach someone on the Northwest baggage line. Busy. Busy. Busy. Finally around 7 P.M., somebody answered the phone. The guy told me my bag was in Chicago. Good news. He said he would be happy to give it to me when I got to the airport. That was at least an hour-and-a-half, away, and an extremely inconvenient proposition in Chicago. So he informed me he could put it in a cab and send it to me, but I would have to pay for the cab. Yes, I would have to pay for the cab if I ever wanted to see my bag again.

Now, I'm willing to admit that such incredible inconvenience can just happen. But I could not grasp how Northwest could treat customers with what appeared to be outright contempt. Maybe the airline could do nothing about the circumstance of weather or the hours of unionized baggage handlers, but even now I wonder what is the least they could have done. For one thing, they could have talked the assembled crowd through the ordeal, not with a canned brush-off (we didn't even get that) but with simple mea culpa human words, like, "I'm sorry you have to go through this and I apologize for the confusion. We will do our best to see that you never have to suffer this kind of thing ever again. Please let us help you with a flight for tomorrow morning when hopefully flying conditions will be better. Our people will not go home until you have had a chance to personally speak to one of them about your options tonight."

I might still have been angry and frustrated, but certainly more willing to give them the benefit of the doubt. That possibility went out the window, however, when the reservations people simply closed shop and went home, which I hoped was to a neighborhood somewhere in Hades.

THE SCREW YOU RULE

What that experience revealed was how an accumulation of seriously negative touchpoints can end in the delivery of a peak moment of overall negative experience. The service people had no authority to do or say anything on their own account. Not one person from management appeared on the scene of what I considered a crisis situation to take charge or accept responsibility. At every turn, the simple power of The Golden Rule was abandoned in favor of The Screw You rule. The hapless front-line staff was left to fend for itself and flounder helplessly in the mess. Where other airlines might have offered conciliatory concessions like a hotel room or a free future flight for those of us who were stranded, what we got was arrogant, often angry disregard. I have no doubt that several hundred frequent flyers lost all faith in Northwest Airlines that night. And as you will discover in this book, it didn't have to be like that.

NORTHWORST

The airline got its start in 1926 as a mail carrier, and it strikes me that it would have been better off to stick with delivering letters and parcels rather than people. At least something with a postage stamp on it doesn't get mad at you, and even if sadly lost will never ask for a refund or a complimentary hotel room. Northwest's fate was sealed when it was absorbed into a merger with Delta to make Delta the world's largest carrier. It continued operating under its own name until full integration into Delta in early 2010. By then, its troubled reputation with travelers had earned it the nickname Northworst Airlines. As the British might say, good riddance to bad rubbish! I say the airline got exactly what it deserved—extinction.

HOW IT WENT FROM NORTHWEST TO NORTHWORST

My friend Mike Bergman worked in marketing at Northwest before and after the merger with Delta, and I asked him to give me a candid appraisal how an airline could go so wrong. Since he now works in the customer experience field for a provider of health care services, he's a good guy to ask this question to, and his answers illustrate useful lessons.

His first observation was that the airline based everything on rational analytics. It was a numbers-driven company whose goal was to optimize things like passenger counts and aircraft layout based on the optimal number of seats in economy versus first class. With any decision, the key question was, "Will this change drive incremental revenue and/ or reduce costs?" The airline based its decision on the assumption that the customer was most interested in—and most willing to pay for—speed and efficiency rather than the comforts of air travel. Thus, most innovation dollars were spent on things like speed of check-in or on-time performance. There was not a significant effort placed on the person-to-person service aspect of air travel. The airport and flight crew management groups absolutely did the best with what they had, but their training dollars were mostly limited to procedure and safety-related items, and their staffing levels were at the absolute minimum. For example, even though delays are inevitable in the airline business, Northwest only staffed for "regular operations" (i.e., on-time performance) and was not willing to invest extra dollars in staff for the inevitable delays and resulting customer service nightmares these produced.

It seems that Northwest management believed that air travel had become a commodity, and thus customers would make their purchase decision based primarily on price and schedule alone. Given this assumption, they believed Northwest had only to be minimally competitive in the "soft" side of air-travel, such as service quality, seat comfort, etc. Customers would not choose Northwest above its competitors even if their customer service was better, so why invest more in it. In a nutshell, Northwest was ruled by operations instead of service, and as a cost culture, not a customer culture. Because of this, the airline's market research and product development departments were some of the first groups to be eliminated during the economic downturn in the early 2000s.

Compounding this fundamental error was a rancorous relationship between the company and the employees and their unions. The long-standing management-labor issue seemed to be a source of low morale, no pride in the work and an attitude of "I don't like this airline. I don't like how they treat me, so why should I go out of my way to do anything for the airline's customers?"

When Mike told me this, it brought back the memory of the attack-dog staff of my Detroit debacle, and I suddenly felt sympathy for the front-desk people on that epic night. Mike's impression of the front-line (he never worked on the front-line) was that they had become embittered against the airline because they reasonably felt uncared for and unvalued. With this, many likely felt little pride in working for Northwest, and may have thought that if travel is painful for the customers, it will in turn be painful for the corporate headquarters staff because they are going to get all the phone calls and nasty letters.

Northwest was one of the first airlines to install self-service kiosks, not for passenger convenience but for saving on labor, as in why pay somebody to help when you can get the customer to do it himself? When the merger happened with Delta, Mike was astonished to see that Delta had spare planes in case of service problems. The list of Northwest's minimum standards went on and on.

There's no better illustration of what can happen to a company, any company, that focuses only on data and operates as a short-sighted money machine, one that does not understand how doing right by its employees and customers is, in the long run, the most efficient way to sustain a profitable business.

INSIGHT—DOING THE RIGHT THING IS THE BEST THING FOR YOUR BUSINESS.

Managing costs is critical, but building loyal customers is your lifeblood—the reason why businesses exist. Doing the right thing for customers is doing the right thing for the business. It is easy to devise ways to cut costs without realizing what those cuts are costing you in the long run. What did the incessant cost cutting at Northwest do for the airline? It cost them their brand and their business. I certainly kept my vow to never fly the airline again. It seems there were many others who felt the same way since Northwest is no more.

Next, let's take a look at a low-cost airline that has earned huge success by doing the right thing and the human thing for employees and customers alike.

CHAPTER 4

How One Airline Turns Little Kindnesses
into One Big Welcome Thing of Joy

FEW COMPANIES IN ANY CATEGORY GET AS MUCH TRUST AND respect for customer care as Southwest Airlines. Even fewer understand that you can't cultivate a never-ending supply of outstanding customer care unless you engage your staff with partnership to make customer care your number one reason for being. Just as one plus one makes two, it follows as the night the day that trust begets internal and external loyalty when you *do the right little things all the time.*

There are few silos at Southwest for the different aspects of running a successful company with 46,000 employees in ninety-seven cities. Every function and employee marches to the same drummer. From accounting to mechanics to reservations to ground and flight crew, there is deep involvement in the art of taking care of customers, and every member of the Southwest community is inculcated into a culture of fun and kindness as a way to enjoy the journey of every working day.

If you need the Southwest Purpose spelled out, it is this: *To connect people to what is important in their lives through friendly, reliable, low–cost air travel.*

I personally think this statement is a bit too humble. If I were asked to rewrite it, I would be presumptuous enough to suggest: *It is the sworn mission of every Southwest employee to bring joy to low–cost air travel one passenger at a time.* As a frequent Southwest passenger, I believe this statement to be the truth, the whole truth and nothing but the truth!

THE PROOF IS IN THE DOING

Stories of unabashed customer care are legend at Southwest. Here are two that illustrate what the airline calls The Southwest Way:

A homeless man wanted to return to his family, and they joyfully booked him a flight on Southwest. His only possession was his much beloved dog, but when he arrived for the flight, he didn't have a pet carrier and could not afford to get one. Without the carrier, he could not board, and he certainly was not going to leave the treasured dog behind, which in turn meant he would not have the pleasure of reuniting with his family. The Southwest pilot heard the man's story and, without hesitation, paid for a carrier out of his own pocket. The remarkable thing was that this kind of spontaneous consideration was in no way unusual, and it was an example of an experience that cannot be part of any kind of manual for how to care for customers. It is the product of an attitude that is deeply embedded in the Southwest culture.

The story might have gone unreported if a family member had not written to give thanks for the return of a brother who had been estranged from them. In other words, the pilot did not make any kind of fuss about his generosity and did not have to seek permission to delay the flight. I'm sure if you asked him, he would say it was nothing more than the right thing to do. He would say it's just The Southwest Way.

It's how a brand's reputation expands, sometimes exponentially, with stories that border on legends.

LIFE AND DEATH

In another extraordinary example, a woman called Southwest to say her husband was desperately racing to the Los Angeles airport to get a flight to Denver, but was stuck in traffic and feared he would miss it. The desperation was that his granddaughter had been the victim of boyfriend abuse and was about to be taken off life support, and the grandfather wanted to be there for the final moment.

Word got to the flight captain. When the man came running from airport security, out of breath with his shoes and his belt in his hand, the pilot was there to meet him and said, "It's okay. I heard your story and we're not going to leave without you."

That pilot had the authority to make such a decision based simply on a culture of caring. Working in that culture, he felt free to delay the fight for one customer without hesitation, and on his own initiative. Southwest's Senior Vice President of Culture and Communication, Ginger Hardage, told me, "Little did we know that the woman who called was a prolific blogger. She blogged the story so well that it went international and was dubbed "Captain Compassion." Because someone did that one little but very important thing that day, it is possible that Southwest gained an untold number of potential passengers. Good deeds get remembered. Good deeds get rewarded. And they are as common everywhere as we care to look. At Southwest, good deeds are numerous daily occurrences that are celebrated within the company for all to share and take pride in, thus perpetuating a mythic habit of what is known internally as "Positively Outrageous Service"—the major ingredient of the Southwest Spirit. And it comes naturally. It reminds me of what poet and musician Lou Reed said about his art: "You do this because you like it, you think what you're making is beautiful. And if you think it's beautiful, maybe they think it's beautiful."

"THERE'S NO CHARGE FOR THAT"

I find delightful encounters with gestures of considerate service everywhere I go. I recently went to visit a friend who lives in a Quebec village a hundred kilometers outside of Montreal. Unpacking my bag, I realized I had forgotten to bring a critical medication. Since I was only there for two days, my friend was sure his local drug store would give me a couple of pills to tide me over. When we went to the store the morning after my arrival, it was obvious that everybody working there knew him, but when he introduced me and explained the situation, the pharmacist said with apology that giving out medication without a prescription could cost her license. She went on, however, to ask me if I knew the phone number of my drug store in Chicago so she could call them for verification. When I did indeed remember the number, she did just that. After a few minutes on the phone, she felt comfortable enough to give me two pills. I offered to pay for the call, but she said it was not necessary. I may never see the inside of that pharmacy ever again, but my friend is a regular and by now he has probably told the story to everybody in the village. He also spoke to the owner with praise for the staff and commended him for his ability to hire the right people. The owner seemed a little mystified that there was anything unusual in the behavior, which is a sure sign that doing the right thing can often come as natural second nature. And an important clue that a commitment to deliver these kind of peak experiences starts at the top.

It's a small example of a peak experience of this brand, but I will remember it forever and it gives me pleasure to tell the story of it. If you ever find yourself in Lac Brome, Quebec, please stop and buy something from Pharmaprix. It's the only drug store within a 20-kilometer radius. And don't worry if you don't speak French; as part of the service, everybody in the store is bilingual.

KINDNESSES ALL COME FROM THE SAME SOURCE

The Southwest pilots' stories and the Pharmaprix story all begin with sympathy for the well-being of someone else. Both pilots and the pharmacist could have said, "Sorry, I can't help you." But I think the way to look at it is this: would you do anything less for a neighbor or a family member? And should not companies treat the customers who provide their living with a little of the same respect? I think the question answers itself: your customer *is* a friend and neighbor, and the difference is only a matter of scale. If we managed our companies of all sizes like mom-and-pop stores, business would be a lot nicer place.

FEELINGS ARE RISKY BUSINESS

You might think that holding up the departure of a plane with more than a hundred passengers on it for the sake of one distressed soul is hardly a small thing. It might even be thought of as a really big deal. But the story illustrates a little thing in the sense that it is a *human* thing. To that one captain, it just felt like the thing to do. And Southwest wants him to trust his feelings. Little caring touchpoints are the product of big caring hearts. They win over the instinctive part of our brain that is only concerned with food, sex, fight or flight, and basic survival that works to keep us safe. Safety is very different from success, from taking chances with other people, from going out on a limb and for doing something for another human just because it feels good. I often read things that stick with me long after I forget the source. One of them is this: *A ship is safe in harbor, but a harbor is never where a ship was meant to be.*

Companies are like people. It's more positively stimulating to slip anchor and get out there in the choppy waters of taking the emotional risk involved in believing people will indeed respond to kindnesses, and that kindness for its own sake is as rewarding for the givers as well as the receivers.

I adore the story of a Spanish-speaking Southwest passenger who was on his way to Houston for a life-saving kidney transplant. Perhaps because of language difficulties, he got off his Southwest flight by mistake in Austin, which meant that by not getting to Houston early the next morning he could miss his chance to get the surgery. A Spanish-speaking gate agent wasted no time figuring out what to do. She called an Austin ramp agent friend she knew who flew his own small plane and lined up a private flight for that evening. She also went along for the ride to make sure their passenger would be more comfortable knowing she was on hand to help with Spanish. Both she and the ramp agent did this on their own authority, which shows how powerful employee empowerment can become when it is truly in place as a no-holds barred right to always doing the right thing.

HOW DOES A COMPANY GET TO BE LIKE SOUTHWEST?

Since its quite humble beginnings in 1971, Southwest has intuitively carved out a competitive advantage in the minds of travelers with the process of employee engagement. I say intuitively because putting employees first and customers at a respected second doesn't sound any more right than putting the cart before the horse, but more and more companies are discovering the good sense of it. Ginger Hardage says, "The way a company behaves on the inside will find its way to the outside. Think of it as a circular motion: happy employees make sure we have happy customers who make sure we have happy shareholders and the cycle continues with that momentum."

This is the momentum of a great company culture. And of course, maintaining such cultural momentum takes constant nurturing day in day out, particularly as the company enjoys the success of getting bigger. This is why Ginger has 148 people working on her culture and communication team alone. Amazingly, the work they do derives much of its inspiration from happy customers who take the time to write in to share their appreciation for the rendering of positively outrageous service – as many as a staggering 30,000 times a year! Their stories are shared with all employees through internal discussions, videos and web interaction. Sometimes Ginger will even invite customers to tell their stories to employees in person.

CEO Gary Kelly does a "shout out" to an employee every week that gets recorded on a phone-in news line and is shared on the internal website. "This week," said Ginger, "the shout out was for an employee in Nashville who picked up on a tweet from a customer saying the only thing that would make the flight better would be a hot breakfast served on a silver platter. So this employee took it on himself to go buy a hot breakfast at McDonald's and meet the customer to surprise her. This is the sort of little story that keeps the meaning of The Southwest Way alive. It's not just pretty words but beautiful action. It's what makes our brand a living entity. It illustrates that our commitment to customer care is the equivalent of a calling."

The question I would ask is, "How likely is it that these little kindnesses create customers for life as well as many others who will hear the stories told?" And when it is an example of a peak experience shared internally, how well does it define the meaning of service to the rest of the company's 46,000 employees beyond the pleasant but standard farewell of "Thank you for flying with us today?" It's a sterling example of the most effective kind of advertising: word of mouth. It's also a sterling example of knowing the critical touchpoints along the route of the customer experience.

I usually explain that you only have to understand the importance of a few of these touchpoints—the most critical moments—but in Southwest's case, they seem to get every one of them right, from the initial contact to the final step off the plane. You can only accomplish this remarkable feat when you marshal every employee in every department behind a common quest so that everybody knows what to do almost by instinct. Every participant understands and is guided by the essential brand story so that it becomes the company leader rather than the guy in the corner office. As you will discover in this book, the energy of the company's brand story and its critical customer touchpoints are the drivers of success in delivering customer experiences that make the difference between success and mediocrity.

My own favorite Southwest tale comes from the time of the 9-11 terror attack when many airlines needed government money to survive the shutdown. Southwest was one of the few that did not require assistance, but *customers actually took it upon themselves to send letters that included checks just in case the airline needed the money!* Ginger verified this as absolutely true, along with stories of employees who volunteered to reduce their pay just to help out! These have to be the most remarkable brand legends ever told. I can think of no other for-profit organization that garners such profound gestures of employee involvement and customer affection.

THE CULTURE COMMITTEE

Employees get included in acts of kindness just as much as customers. The 200-member Culture Committee conducts Culture Blitz events every year. On a designated day, the Culture Committee will meet different flights and surprise the attendants by bringing them food and cleaning the plane for them so they can take a break. The team will cook breakfast for the maintenance folks because their shifts change so early in the day. The team will also leave surprises, like new break-room furniture or a gas grill for department cookouts. At least one third of the entire organization gets covered every year with these kinds of blitzes. They are examples of how peak experiences can include employees as well as customers.

In addition to visits from the CEO, the company has a program called "Location Visits" in which a department head adopts a city for two years at a time. The director of maintenance, for example, will adopt a city like Jacksonville that doesn't even have a maintenance department to be on hand for things like location anniversaries and other special events.

And a sense of employee ownership is encouraged with a fabulous profit-sharing plan in which the company matches every employee's 401K contribution. When pilots look for safe ways to save fuel, they do so for what it means to the company and their fellow Southwest coworkers. Airlines work with extremely thin margins, so a penny saved in operations is indeed a penny earned. One flight attendant saw that Southwest trash bags had the airline's logo printed on them. She suggested that it did not help anybody to make something special out of garbage. When this printing procedure was discontinued, it saved $300,000 a year. It's the kind of initiative that comes about when a company takes the time to make employees business literate and dollar vigilant. Southwest does this very well as a part of inculcating a caring attitude about the company's welfare for the benefit of all. Employee involvement in this process takes carefully packaged information put together in appetizing ways as stories. One way Southwest does it is through an employee blog and weekly television show.

THE LAW OF NATURAL SELECTION

When a position becomes available at Southwest, it is posted on line for usually no more than twenty-four hours before it is filled with applications galore. The recruitment qualities looked for are "a warrior's spirit, a servants heart, and a fun-luving attitude." After extensive interviewing against these criteria (and aren't they fabulous!), no new employee starts without attending what is called Fly Class as part of a comprehensive Employee Orientation and Onboarding program. A series of speakers help them understand the brand and what it stands for. There's a party afterwards hosted by a different department every week. And no employee is ever allowed to forget the customer-care promise every day of their employment. It's revealing that what we normally call Human Resources is known at Southwest as the People Department. This small touchpoint in the employee experience speaks wonders for those who hate thinking of themselves either as a "resource" or anything other than a bona fide member of the team!

Every February, CEO Kelly travels to different cities to deliver his annual message at the Southwest Rally. Employees can come in and ask questions of him and hear great stories. In 2012, he was able to connect in person with 11,000 employees directly. There is also a video series in which any employee can ask him a question in a video shot using his or her own smart phone. Some of these questions and his answers are made into a weekly newscast for what is known as SWA TV, so through the Internet any employee can log on.

IT'S ABOUT COMMUNITY

It is clear that Southwest people feel themselves to be members of their own community a little like a clan or tribe. But it's a sense of community that gets shared with the larger communities outside the brand. As a 40th anniversary celebration, the company organized a tour with the Student Conservation Association in forty communities across the country. Southwest customers were invited to join environmental cleanups and hundreds showed up.

The use of social media also helps keep the community spirit alive. Houston's Hobby Airport, for example, was only a domestic airport until Southwest petitioned city council to make it international. The company started a web site called "Free Hobby" in which customers and associations Southwest had supported over the years joined in to get the project (excuse the pun) off the ground. It worked.

BE OF GOOD CHEER ALL YE WHO ENTER HERE.

Flying with Southwest is renowned as a fun experience. Empowered employees feel free to enjoy their passengers as partners in the experience. Cabin crews have casual dress options. Every flight attendant is given a fun book with a section on good jokes, games to play and songs to sing, which is why they've been known to burst into song. Nobody has to use it if it does not fit his or her personal style. Everybody is encouraged to find his or her own way. Southwest does not want clones, and this emphasis on finding the *best you* is what makes flying the airline such a pleasure that runs throughout the entire organization. As the airline's director of in-flight training says, "Everybody is expected to color *outside* the lines."

Even some of the advertising lines I remember from over the years do this. My favorite is "The somebody else up there who loves you." Another is "You're now free to move about the country." And the one I find most fitting: "Just Plane Smart."

IMITATION IS THE BEST FORM OF FLATTERY

You can never adopt the inherent quality of another brand's culture, but you can adopt a brand's business model. Many other airlines have tried to achieve Southwest's amazing results by imitating the company's high level of employee engagement. Canada's popular Westjet and Europe's Ryan Air are just two from around the world that have played copycats. A Westjet Christmas video that went viral suggests they also share the same ethic: Santa appears on a television screen in an airport departure terminal. He speaks directly to passing passengers and asks them what they want for Christmas. I'm not sure how it was done, but he even knows everybody's name. The requests are duly noted, but here's the truly amazing thing: while the passengers were in the air, the Westjet ground crew at the destination rushed out to buy *all* the requested gifts and had them wrapped and sent down the carousel with the customer's luggage. Each package had the passengers name on it and the gifts were exactly what each passenger ordered. One ordered a laptop. Another asked for a big-screen TV. One guy who thought it was a joke had ordered socks and underwear. To their astonishment and delight, every passenger on that Westjet flight got exactly what they asked for, and I bet the guy who asked for socks and underwear is kicking himself to this day! The last time I checked You Tube, the video of this amazing customer experience had been viewed nearly 40 million times. That's not a typo. It's 40,000,000 times. Check it out by typing in Westjet Christmas miracle on the You Tube search bar.

KINDNESS PAYS

Southwest has been profitable for the past forty-two years and is now the nation's largest domestic airline in terms of customers carried (120 million every year) with a reputation for being the most trusted and most profitable of all the airlines. The "most profitable" part of that equation proves without a doubt that understanding the importance of critical touchpoints in the customer experience is paramount. For Southwest's workers, we see that all their focus and energy is directed toward delivering sensitive little moments that form a customer memory bank that defines the overall experience. Spontaneous gestures are the foundation of the airline's caring business practice and its well-earned success.

A LOVE BRAND

If it is possible to love a brand with passion, this is the one. It is the brand I would most want to marry my daughter! That's because I see kindness as love's closest relative. It never fails to impress me. And kindness is newsworthy. Reports of customers driving up to the order window of a fast-food chain are told more and more, "your food was paid for by the last customer." It's called "paying forward." In some places it has become contagious enough to make the nightly news broadcast. In Canada's ubiquitous Tim Horton's restaurant chain, the phenomenon recently went viral. A New York Times story reported 10,000 "paid forward" coffees were bought in twenty-eight locations in a very short period of time. One anonymous customer arranged with a Tim Horton's manager to buy 500 coffees at their drive-through window!

Getting a little gift like that can really make your day. It can make you see strangers as not very strange at all. Little kindnesses can indeed become contagious, and when practiced inside a company as they are at Southwest, they inspire the entire team and become a reason for being.

Kindness is the world's most underrated gift. As reported by The Associated Press, author George Saunders wrote a Syracuse University graduation speech that went viral on blogs and social networks and is now being turned into a book. "Who in your life do you remember most fondly with the most undeniable feelings of warmth?" he asks. "Those who were kindest to you, I bet."

He goes on to say, the "failures of kindness" are "those moments when another human being was there, in front of me, suffering, and I responded … sensibly. Reservedly. Mildly. It's a little facile, and certainly hard to implement, but I'd say as a goal in life you could do worse than: Try to be kinder."

The only part of that argument the people at Southwest would argue with is that kindness is hard to implement. For them, it is simply a way of life. I urge you to fly this airline every chance you get. It will help you to discover how keenly employees are drawn to work that matters. In fact, 71 percent of Southwest employees describe their job as a "calling." Most certainly they will willingly work hard for money, but at Southwest they even more willingly work for meaning. You can bet that, given a reason to believe, this would be true for employees in many more companies, including yours.

INSIGHT–KNOW HOW YOUR COMPANY MAKES PEOPLE FEEL.

Providing a great customer experience is a *human thing*. Employees and customers are people who run on emotions. Your company is a dynamic emotional ecosystem; every small action creates a feeling that ripples throughout the entire environment. When management truly cares for employees, employees *feel* good about themselves and empowered to make customers *feel* cared for. Creating an environment for an extraordinary customer experience is not something you do. You *feel it and live it*. Your company's emotional ecosystem is nurtured and sustained with your culture. When you do it right, like Southwest does, the brand's ecosystem becomes a virtuous cycle, or as my colleague Christian Lauffer says, "When the brand achieves Nirvana, the company and the customers care for each other equally."

CHAPTER 5

A Word About the Word "Culture"

HEAVEN IS WHERE THE COOKS ARE FRENCH, THE LOVERS ARE Italian, the police are British and everything is organized by the Swiss.

Hell, on the other hand, is where the cooks are British, the lovers Swiss, the mechanics French and everything is organized by the Italians.

This old joke has in it grains of truth as we perceive the myths of these countries. I call them myths because they are so easily perpetuated as stories, and just as countries are defined by cultural stories, so are smaller communities from towns and villages down to families and the places where we work. Cultures have memories and a history of stories that are told time and time again until they practically become fact.

When you think of companies as communities in their own right, their cultures become the defining factor in how they behave and how we perceive them, and their products as stories we tell ourselves and others. The prescient Peter Drucker told us all years ago, "Culture eats strategy." This was not well understood way back then, but it was a warning that all the fine data metrics and strategic planning in the world do little good if employees are not clued in and eager to support a defined cause. This explains why the more we think about what brands mean to employees and customers, the more we see the word "culture" popping up so frequently in contemporary brand analysis. You will see it sprinkled liberally throughout this book, and because we should never,

ever take it for granted, I hope you won't find it too boring if I take a minute to explore what "culture" actually means.

HOITY TOITY

Somewhere along the line, the word culture became associated with the arts and as something lofty and intellectual beyond the reach of ordinary people. But the concept of culture becomes more accessible if we think of it not as something vague and distant, but in terms of unique traits that are born of innate character in people and their organizations. Everybody has a character whether he or she likes it or not, and so does every company. Just think of the difference between the cultures of Southwest Airlines and Northwest Airlines as a vivid example.

The personality that emerges from your innate character represents your identity to the world just as the way your company behaves and reveals what it is like as if it were a person. This is why quite often in customer research we ask people who a brand would be if it were a person. The question reveals that culture is more about emotions than it is about facts. As Tony Hsieh, CEO of Zappos, says in his book *Delivering Happiness:*

> *For individuals, character is destiny.*
> *For organizations, culture is destiny.*

Think about somebody you admire. I bet it has to do with that person's character. For example, you can't quantify how an actor like Tom Hanks makes you feel, but it says a great deal about how he makes a lot of people feel when a couple of years ago a popular opinion poll nominated him as the most trusted man in America (I'll resist the urge to comment on what this says about the state of our culture). If Tom were a brand, the brand would be characterized as a culture of trust. He would have to do something really awful for people to change their minds.

While not impossible, it's very difficult for you to change. With all the good intentions in the world, you tend to get stuck with who you are. This could be something to do with being naturally introverted or extraverted, shy or bold. In the case of the Chinese, it's cultural: they simply do not smile at strangers and probably think we westerners are all grinning idiots. If a Chinese woman smiles, even when she is with an acquaintance, she covers her mouth for fear of offending.

In any event, you might try to change yourself, but don't try to change other people. It simply doesn't work. What you can do, however, is work with who and what they are and how their talents (and limitations) can best be put to work for mutual advantage. Some people respond very badly to criticism, so you adjust the way you speak with them to take that into account. Others you can joke with and speak candidly. It's all a part of recognizing differences and adapting to them. It is also unavoidable to not have favorite people simply because you are hopefully as human as anybody else. The one thing we all have in common, however, is the joy we find in doing work that matters in an environment of internal and external respect.

CHANGE IS HARD

The way a brand starts is usually the way it will finish in our consciousness. Take a relatively inexpensive car brand like Hyundai. In its early iterations it got a reputation for being cheaply made rather than just being inexpensive, and while the brand's quality has improved a thousand-fold over the thirty or so years after its initial entry into North America, at least among older people it unjustly continues to carry a little of the old stigma. A brand can move down in our estimation but it's hard for it to move up. The Hyundai Sonata is rated at the top of the J.D. Powers quality index and the entire line of its cars is also highly rated. But while Hyundai has earned the right to a good spot in our estimations, it will never be equated with the likes of a Mercedes-Benz even if it ever wanted to. This has nothing to do with the fact that many luxury cars like Mercedes and BMW rate below Hyundai for reliability and duration of warranty. Affordability and luxury are based on different cultural myths that affect the way we feel about our cars and every other product we invite into our lives. Hyundai's carefully evolved quest is to produce good, reliable, affordable cars. This is the definition of the Hyundai brand and the driver of its considerable success. Even its very fine luxury model is sold as a less expensive alternative to the prestigious marques. Would making it more expensive have moved the entire brand's perception up in the world? It's not a bad question, but higher price is not in cultural character for the Hyundai brand.

We usually associate culture with something positive, but a culture can also be toxic. If you have ever worked in a company with a toxic culture, you know what damage it can do to your self-esteem. Such companies are often led by charismatic personalities who take up too much time and attention away from what is essential. You can spot toxic charisma very easily. Those who have it suck all the air out of the room the moment they walk in. Avoid them whenever you can.

PEDIGREE

Like many other great brands, Southwest's cultural identity begins with the innate values of its founder and legendary first CEO, Herb Kelleher. It's easy to imagine him as a capable, generous and happy soul who would seem to believe that life lived according to the Golden Rule is the only way to go. It's not something that can be faked. The airline seems to have a genuinely intuitive desire to take good care of the emotional well-being of its employees, which in turn is an astute way to make sure they will take care of their passengers who become habitual in making the airline so successful. The unique culture of Southwest is inextricably bound by this covenant.

I met Herb once at a dinner on the floor of the New York Stock Exchange in honor of his nomination as CEO Of The Year by *Chief Executive* magazine. When I told him how much I love Southwest people, he said, "I'm very proud that our people are friendly and smile because they want to, not because I told them to." I'm sure Herb is completely right about that, but my suspicion is that he probably looked for people who found it very easy to smile when he first started the airline and the habit caught on. I read recently that when he was asked about his role in teaching caring behavior to Southwest people, he said, "I didn't teach them; their parents did!"

The qualities a founder brings to a brand in its nascent form are probably the ones that will stick for good or bad to be developed as the brand matures. Only a lot of time and the inculcation of a new ethic will ever change our perception of it. You can't just willy-nilly import another culture any more than Germans can suddenly become Hawaiians.

Can you imagine our German friends suddenly dressing in grass skirts and hibiscus leis instead of lederhosen and hiking boots while blasting out "Deutschland Uber Alles" with a thunderous band of ukuleles instead of oompah brass?

This is why companies that need a makeover can learn from what other companies do, but only cherry pick what they can use from other cultures to improve their own. You can't copy culture. It has to be real and stand for something meaningful. If it's not authentic, people will know, and it won't survive let alone thrive. Still, understanding what other successful cultures do is a good way to find ideas and get tips for what works and how to get the ball rolling (and who knows how many Germans might love to give up ungainly trombones and tubas in favor of the cute little uke!).

START WITH LITTLE THINGS

A little thing like senior leadership getting a few people out for a casual lunch could include asking what they think is right with the company and in what ways it can be improved, and then implementing the good suggestions. Employees may not feel free to be completely candid, but at least the leaders show a willingness to start a dialogue that could be the precursor to sending out a request for opinions with a pledge of anonymity. If you do not have company picnics, start them. If you run a factory, walk around and talk to people. Surprise people with random acts of recognition and remember that all good intentions start with good manners. If your parking lot has its spaces delineated by order of rank, make it completely random with first-come, first-served to show democracy is alive and well in your workplace. Steal the free ice cream wagon in the parking lot idea from a wonderful company you will read about in the next chapter. Share stories of employees who understand the meaning of delivering outstanding customer experience. Sharing such stories works better than any kind of formal manual simply because live example works better than static dialogue (as you will see, many of the companies featured in this book do this with great effectiveness). Start a company band and give lunchtime concerts in the cafeteria. Hey, you could bring in a ukulele teacher to give lessons on a dozen free instruments. Get a nurse in to give free flu shots to help minimize sick days off the job. You will indeed discover that little things you do mean more than big things you say, and it takes very little imagination to get them going as a way to build trust and confidence in the workforce.

Taking the norm of eight hours a day, you will probably spend at least 27 years of your life at work. It's healthy to think that most of them can be lived with large portions of enjoyment, of sharing, of caring, of stimulating connection to something worthwhile besides the same amount of time in your lifetime you will spend lying in bed!

None of the companies featured in this book started out with every detail of its culture in place. Cultures are probably best developed by what has been called *continuous deployment*, which is a fancy way of saying baby steps. It's all the little things that eventually add up to helping each member of your corporate family to develop his and her full potential. This, in the long run, is what a positive culture is all about: people feel—and are—truly important when they get a sense of the value of their contribution, and customers naturally gravitate toward companies that feel genuine concern for their welfare and experience.

Further, when you investigate what the word culture means in terms of customer experience as defined in this book, you may indeed discover that *culture is everything and the only thing* that separates the men from the boys in terms of unmitigated customer experience success, and that the art of it can indeed be learned and absorbed by establishing a core cultural values story as *the* reason for being. This is what Tony Hseieh did at Zappos to create the phenomenon we will talk about later.

Going back to the beginning of this chapter, as a matter of curiosity, France did not come from a culture of culinary excellence all by itself. A red-blooded Frenchman would probably go to war to guard that reputation, but at the risk of bursting a cultural bubble, I happen to know that a Florentine named Catherine de Medici brought the art of great food preparation to France when she went to the French court during the Renaissance. It was an Italian who taught the French to cook! This is what I mean when I say a very fine cultural myth can indeed be born by picking cherries.

LESSON LEARNED—YOUR CULTURE REVEALS YOUR TRUE CHARACTER

Culture is everything. It embodies your company's reason for being. Your culture reveals your company's character, integrity and competence. It lays bare whether or not you can be trusted. When companies fail to create cultures that are genuinely concerned for their employees, customers will sense the company doesn't care about them either.

A positive culture, focused on things that matter, things that improve the human condition, makes people feel connected to something greater than themselves. Something meaningful that we want and need to be part of because it makes us feel that much better about our own contributions to the greater good.

CHAPTER 6

High Tech, High Touch: How to be a Cognoid

ASK A DOZEN CEO'S WHAT THEY THINK THEIR COMPANIES DO BEST and I'll bet you ten bucks more than half of them will give you a very animated account of the bottom line and its return on investment to shareholders.

Not Robert Willett.

As CEO of Cognex, he undoubtedly thinks a lot about finances, but what excites him is his company's successful culture.

I include his story in this book because it is the perfect example of how to lead and build a wildly successful company from the inside out, and how it is done with vibrant internal content that is celebrated by 1,100 universally motivated employees in twenty countries around the world.

Cognex stands for "cognition experts." Founded by Dr. Robert Shillman in the early 1980s, it was one of the first companies to explore commercial machine vision applications – literally teaching machines to see and discriminate.

Says CEO Willett, "Dr. Bob is a guy with huge drive and vision and right off the bat he saw the value of creating a company where it would be forever great fun to come to work every day. He imagined a company where 'work hard, play hard and move fast' becomes the everyday mantra, one where you don't just *like* coming to work, you *love* it, and you love it well enough to call yourself a Cognoid."

Mixing high jinks fun with high tech work sounds like an oxymoron, but as Willett says, "Just because we are serious about the quality of our technology does not mean we have to be serious about ourselves." And he kids you not:

THE SARAH PALIN CAPER

Imagine assembling several hundred people in the cafeteria at the company's headquarters in Natick, Massachusetts, to hear a surprise speech by Sarah Palin. A local police escort chaperones her limo to the front door. She is introduced with great fanfare and considerable surprise.

Regardless of their politics, people are amazed to see her. Sarah explains she is talking to local business leaders about how to get our economy "back up on its hind legs and roarin' like a mama grizzly." Slowly but surely, however, as her speech progresses, some in the audience come to see that it is *not Sarah.* It is a talented actor doing a Sarah impersonation! By the time people catch on to the joke, Dr, Bob explains how Cognex is doing its part for the economy by giving each employee a $100 gift card and the afternoon at the Mall to spend it however they choose.

This is how one thoughtful little event can create an endearing memory to last a lifetime.

THE GURU SPEECH

On another occasion, a highly touted marketing expert and motivational speaker came to address the assembled staff. Dr. Bob introduced him with great accolade as he recited his impressive credentials before joining the audience to receive the speaker's pearls of wisdom.

After about ten minutes of nothing but vapid clichéd nonsense, Dr. Bob leaned over to his neighbor and whispered loudly, *"God, this guy is boring."*

He had purposely left on his remote microphone!

The place totally cracked up as the audience realized they had been had once again, and that the phony speech was nothing more than the preamble to another fun company event, what they call a "play day"—a surprise afternoon off for all employees—usually to an off-site destination like an amusement park or the aquarium—but sometimes employees stay on site to have a picnic, games and a field day on the property surrounding the company's headquarters. On-site events are called "stay days."

CEO Willett takes obvious pleasure in these stories and many more like them. On Halloween, everybody gets dressed up in elaborate costumes and it is not unusual to see top execs in drag. On a hot summer day an internal e-mail might appear on everybody's computer screen saying ice cream is now being served in the parking lot, and when people show up it is Dr. Bob doing the serving from a real ice cream truck dressed in a crisply pressed Good Humor ice cream man's outfit. At a financial meeting with employees in Shanghai, guys dressed up in inflatable Disney-like costumes suddenly appear for a fun sumo-wrestling contest. When you drive up to the company entrance, a sign pointing left says *Work Hard*—an arrow pointing right on the same sign says *Play Hard*. On the left is the company's headquarters. On the right is a two-acre sport field where on any given day you might see dozens of Cognoids playing Ultimate Frisbee.

THE COST OF CULTURE

Every year Cognex allocates about 13 percent of its revenue ($48 million in 2013) to research and development to keep its technology ahead of the curve, but funds spent on the care and feeding of the culture are considered an equally important investment. Remarkably, eleven of Cognex's largest offices, from Massachusetts to Budapest to Shanghai, have a Minister of Culture who takes this job on as a responsibility. Senior managers are also assessed on how well they embrace the culture and it is calculated into their compensation reviews. All of this just goes to prove that there's more to a culture of fun than a few giggles.

THE SERIOUS SIDE OF FUN

No company exists to simply entertain its workers. All the Cognex comedy and crazy antics serve a purpose: Playing together creates a sense of community, a sense of belonging. It breaks down barriers between people to encourage familiarities that are the foundation of trust in any community.

We are a social species, and companies are by their very nature social as well as commercial units. It's just plain human to want to be with people you like and with whom you know you can be yourself. Familiarity doesn't breed contempt; it's much more likely to build trust and cooperation. Having a good laugh is a good way to get there. Cognex delivers in spades.

OPEN FOR BUSINESS

The company's commitment to "taking work seriously but not ourselves" breaks barriers between staff and management to propagate open communication. Nobody is on a high horse. The "boss" you can laugh with is the "boss" you can trust to ask difficult questions and one you can go to for help when you need it. I put the word boss in quotation marks because the more you talk to Robert Willett, the more you realize that the real boss at Cognex is the Cognex culture itself.

"DON'T DO WHAT YOU'RE TOLD. DO WHAT'S RIGHT."

This is a clearly stated position put to all Cognex employees at all levels. Management might want an engineer to solve a problem a certain way. If the engineer sees it differently, he is duty-bound to speak up. This very often produces better results than if the engineer had followed orders. The old command-and-control ethic of the industrial revolution is long dead. When Cognoids come up with successful solutions that go against what was asked for, they are publicly presented with the Do What's Right award—a framed $100-dollar bill signed by the founder and the CEO. As Robert Willett says, "Very smart capable people who are passionate about what they do are also likely to be irreverent skeptics who ask 'why.' This is an essential part of an open culture. Questioning decisions is the healthy thing to do."

Smart, capable, highly-educated people have portable skills and know that the company needs them as much as the other way around. They also have feet, and when the feet get itchy, they know how to move them to what might be a greener pasture. You don't pay people to agree with you.

YES-MEN NEED NOT APPLY

When you empower and require people to think for themselves and speak without fear, *everybody* in your company becomes a leader. What we carelessly call the "rank and file" gets the message. Give everybody a chance to be a winner and they will seek out opportunities to prove it. Robert Willet does not look for passengers. What he encourages is a plane full of pilots all wanting to fly in the same direction.

He even encourages uncomfortable questions. Every quarter he has an Ask the President meeting where people in every Cognex office all over the world can submit anonymous questions. Then in a beer-and-pizza evening, the questions get answered by senior management and a transcript of the event is made available to all Cognoids on the company intranet site.

Says Willett: "There are no sacred cows. It's like the Town Hall meeting where everything is out in the open. Like 'why aren't our raises bigger?' Or 'what are you doing about a competitor's product we're worried about?' For many CEOs, it's tempting not to want to hear that stuff. Or it's tempting to want to control it and not have everybody hear it publicly. But the benefits of transparency far exceed the risks. It puts everybody in the same boat so that problems aren't allowed to fester into something bigger than they really are. Sometimes it even helps senior people to come to grips with problems they did not know existed. I think everybody appreciates the intent."

IT'S NOT A COMPANY; IT'S A TRIBE

You can imagine that as an employee you could *align* yourself with this company. As Laurence D. Ackerman said in *Identity Is Destiny*, organizations are inherently relational and "relationships are only as strong as the natural alignment between the identities of the participants."

I love this thought. It explains to me how flaws in that natural alignment are why we often have troubled relationships with our teenagers who are desperately trying to find their own identity, why many corporate mergers seemingly made in heaven are difficult to manage, how many companies fail to reach their full potential and even why marriages fail. Get the natural alignments right between *all* the players in your company and you create *a tribe of champions.* Champions love doing what is right rather than doing what they are told. Champions have fire in the belly. Champions turn no into yes. And everybody loves a champion.

POWERFUL TRIBES PROSPER WITH AN INFECTIOUS ESPRIT DE CORPS

The 101st Airborne Division has an invincible spirit. So does the US Marine Corps and its allied Navy Seals. Only very special people can take on the rigor and pace set by these kinds of organizations. They attract the best because what they do is hard to do. And most important, they *care* about each other. They have each other's back. And this becomes a powerful kind of faith.

Every dedicated member takes pride in bearing his or her collective identity as a symbol of specialness in much the same way that the 101st Airborne takes pride in the eagle so colorfully stitched onto its shoulder patch. The collective is only as powerful as every one of the individuals involved. It's easy to see how viral this kind of spirit can be to potential recruits and customers alike. If you have ever once had this experience of being a citizen in a tribe of champions, you can never go back to the ordinary alternative, which is a lack of tribal pride, a lack of caring, a lack of faith and a loser tribe of lost souls. As they say in the Marine Corps, "Once a Marine, always a Marine." It is more than coincidence that the Marine Corps motto is "Semper Fidelis."

YOU CAN TAKE IT TO THE BANK

Robert Willett looks upon his company as a 33-year-old, 350-million-dollar startup, which is an essential attitude for staying fresh, motivated and free from bureaucracy. It also reaps enviable financial gain with gross margins of 75 percent in a business that is enjoying equally enviable growth. Willett sees this as a testament to the value his customers see in Cognex people and products. The enthusiasm of a team installing a robot in a customer's factory is just as important as the work the robot actually does. As Seth Godin says in *All Marketers Tell Stories*, "... irrational beliefs aren't a distraction – they are an intrinsic part of the quality of the product."

Go to a restaurant that serves great food with indifferent service and the food doesn't matter. The same principle applies to an encounter with a bank manager, a flight attendant, a doctor's appointment or any encounter your company's people have with a customer. Guard it with your life. I once heard a hotel manager chide a front-desk clerk for telling a guest, "That's not my job." The manager said, "Anything that customer wants is your job. Without his happiness, you have no job."

AND IT'S ALL IN THE FAMILY

When a child is born to a Cognoid, it is called a Coggler. If that is not charming enough, every Coggler gets five shares of Cognex stock and a stuffed bear wearing a shirt that says "Cognex Loves You." Cognoids work hard not because they have to, but because they want to. Long hours are often the price paid by families, so family days are celebrated with pool parties and other outings and no Coggler is left behind. Perseverance is also rewarded at various stages along length of time on the job. For example, after thirty years of service, every Cognoid gets $25,000 to invest and donate to the charity of his or her choice.

AGAIN, IT'S THE LITTLE THINGS

You can't help but notice that much of what goes on at Cognex are little things. Fun little things. Caring little things. Recognition little things. Kind little things. And always human little things. They work piece by piece to form a cohesive whole—a gestalt, to use a fancy word—that is way bigger than the sum of its parts.

Giving somebody who leaves the company and then comes back a beautiful Australian aboriginal boomerang in a case that says "I like Cognex so much I joined twice," for just one example, is a little thing that speaks volumes not only to the returnee but to every single person in the tribe. So is spending time and money on "play days." And the list goes on in highly imaginative, thoughtful ways that are far from rote incentives.

CAN YOU DO IT, TOO?

If your company does half of what Cognex does, you are creating an uncommon sense of self-worth, belonging and enthusiasm that translate into emotional bounty for your customers. But be careful; it requires a sense of doing the right thing, because doing the right thing is the only thing. If what you do smells of ulterior motive, it just doesn't work. I said earlier that Cognex is like a person you would want to know and trust. It's a matter of authenticity. If Cognex were not *naturally* inclined to be the company that it is, all the fun and games would smell like week-old fish. If you do not mean it from the bottom of your heart, don't even try it. As the saying goes, the road to Hell is paved with good intentions!

You might, however, find enough inspiration in this book's stories to create the kind of culture that can be unique to your business. Your company has a culture just as surely as your brand has a personality, whether you like it or not. The nature of both is not seen in a grand mission statement pinned on your boardroom wall, but (and you might get sick of hearing me say this) in the little things you do day in and day out to keep your business going. If you can cherry pick from what has been successful for others, why not? I find that most good brand leaders are students of what other brands do. Whatever they can teach is insightful manna to be used wisely.

CEO AS SPIRITUAL LEADER

Robert Willett would undoubtedly blush and perhaps protest at the above subhead. But all through our chat it is clear that he relishes and nurtures his role as the keeper of the Cognex faith. He concerns himself with what it *feels* like to be a Cognoid, and he fiercely protects and nurtures that feeling. The technology might be complex, but so is the emotional feel and touch of the brand. To the future of Cognex and its staff, that emotional content is more priceless than all the company's investment in plant and equipment. It is the lifeblood of its success. And just think: what if founder Dr. Bob and the CEO Willett did *not* see the necessity of nurturing a dynamic culture? What if all they thought about was making money and to heck with fun, to heck with spending on R&D and to heck with caring how employees feel?

I think we all know the answer to that one. One of the most significant remarks Robert made during my interview with him was this: "We decided we would rather have a small group of Cognoids and be committed to maintaining the culture than cutting out all of what makes Cognex special."

It has become a marketing truism to say that it costs more to get a new customer than to keep an old one. Robert would probably add that it costs more to hire a new employee than to keep a good one. Very few people leave Cognex because a lot of time is spent getting the right fit for the culture. Example: an open senior position recently involved reviewing nearly 500 candidates over nine months before it was filled! Figuring out the right fit costs a lot less than fixing a mistake.

After my chat with Robert, I thought how great it would be to go get a PhD in electrical engineering so I could maybe get a job at Cognex. Then it occurred to me: the best thing about that absurd idea how is big a laugh it would get from all 1,100 Cognoids.

LESSON LEARNED–LEAD FROM YOUR HEART.

Sir Richard Branson, of Virgin fame, kindly contributed the foreword to my book, *Emotional Branding.* His words still ring true today. Here's a bit of his wisdom:

"The idea that a business is strictly a numbers affair has always struck me as preposterous. For one thing, I have never been particularly good at numbers, but I think I've done a reasonable job with feelings. And I'm convinced that it is feelings — and feelings alone — that account for the success of the Virgin brand in all its myriad forms.

"It is my conviction that what we call 'shareholder value' is best defined by how strongly employees and customers feel about your brand. Nothing seems more obvious to me that a product or service only becomes a brand when it is imbued with profound values that can translate into fact and feeling that employees can project and customers can embrace.

"By profound, I mean simple. Everybody appreciates being treated decently. Everybody admires honesty. Everybody believes in excellence and value. Everybody likes to have fun and to feel part of something bigger than himself.

"These values shape my rather simple view of business, but they are (or should be) universal, which is why I find it astonishing that it has taken so long to capture such a view between the covers of a business book."

If you have any doubt that leading from the heart is the right way to run a business, just consider the high performing success of Cognex or any of the 400 Virgin Group companies. We should all recognize the brilliance of Dr. Bob and Robert Willet, and subscribe enthusiastically to the wisdom of Sir Richard's determinations: a business is always more about feelings rather than numbers if it wants to achieve maximum success.

CHAPTER 7

What This Country Needs is
an Honest Bottle of Tea

WITH THE PROLIFERATION OF NEW PRODUCTS COMING ON THE market every year, only those that offer a significant difference are likely to get a shot at success. While this little nugget might seem like the product of common sense, it was impressed upon me by Seth Godin in one of his brilliant little books called *The Purple Cow*. In a field full of brown cows, says Seth, a purple cow will stand out to command your attention. To survive and prosper in the sea of new products that come on the market every year, make sure you invent a purple cow.

Another Seth by the name of Seth Goldman, along with his partner Barry Nalebuff, wrote a purple cow kind of book called *Mission In A Bottle: The Honest Guide to Doing Business Differently and Succeeding.* It tells the saga of how with the right idea and motivation, you can invent a stand-out product that cuts itself out from the me-too herd, and being different can help overcome the incredible obstacles that face you in taking your new baby from concept to market.

What makes their book so different is that it's told in comic book form with illustrations by Sungyoon Choi. It is literally the purple cow of business books that tells how Seth and Barry successfully invented a new thirst-quencher.

MUTUAL ADMIRATION

Seth was Barry's student at the Yale School of Management when the idea for a different kind of bottled drink first came up as a class exercise. Later, in 1997, after a run in Central Park, Seth found himself thirsty but couldn't find anything besides water that he wanted to drink. This is when he called Barry in New Haven to renew the discussion about a drink that would be different because it was not loaded with too much sugar or chemical sweetener. Back in New Haven when Seth was a student, the two had been playing with orange juice mixed with club soda, but the idea of a new kind of drink took greater hold in their minds when Barry suggested it could be something healthy like tea in a bottle without all the sugar in teas already on the market. He came up with the name Honestea.

THE MISSIONARY INSTINCT

As a PhD business professor and consultant, Barry knew a lot about economics and marketing, while after graduation Seth started out in the nonprofit and socially-responsible business sectors. He went the nonprofit route because he thought it would give him the opportunity to do his bit to change the world for the better. He was committed to social entrepreneurship and quickly saw that Honestea could combine social and business entrepreneurship for achieving the same kind of results one might expect from a nonprofit whose quest was to improve the American diet.

They knew little about the beverage industry, but had a strong gut feeling that the Honestea idea would work, and it fit well into their belief that business can be a powerful tool for change.

After a trademark investigation, they found Honestea was in conflict with Nestea. Separating the two words into Honest Tea seemed like a simple solution and perhaps less gimmicky.

HOW SWEET IT ISN'T

Barry had been to India to write a case study on the Tata Tea Company. The experience made him see that he had been drinking bad tea all his life and that the new product would have greater chance for success if it were made with the really good stuff. The guys decided to experiment on their friends. They mixed up batches of tea with different levels of sugar content.

The average bottled tea comes with a whopping 12 teaspoons of sugar in a 16-oz. bottle. Talk about read my hips! But people making their iced tea at home usually add only two teaspoons with no loss of taste. This conformed to the economic theory of "declining marginal utility." Honest Tea was off to a good start in concept form, but a long way from where they were destined to grow, to more than 100 million bottles a year!

WHO DOES WHAT

Seth and Barry divvied up responsibilities. Seth took on the CEO job (he calls it Tea-EO) while Barry took on the job of chairman and making Seth successful by contributing ideas and helping raise capital, which could be done while he continued his work at Yale. Seth, on the other hand, decided he had to go all-in with a do-or-die commitment to the project. He took the giant step of quitting his job to go with a wing and a prayer and no back-up plan into a venture that might fly or drop like a stone. He figured the only way to ensure the flying part was to have faith in himself, his partner and the efficacy of their combined intent to give the world something different. This is the way of the passionate entrepreneur. This is the ship that goes to sea because it is boring to feel safe in the harbor. It takes a sense of business artistry, not just business sense, to follow such a course to success. As the ancient saying goes, "Faint heart never won fair maiden."

THE PLAN

Seth was never interested in creating a me-too product. It had to be one that would make a difference in people's lives. Tea was healthy to begin with, and with the right added ingredients for superior flavor, he knew that Honest Tea would be attractive to large numbers of people who care enough about their health to read labels. He summed it up in a business plan that would be the guiding star of what he knew could be the brand's journey on the way to success:

> Honest Tea seeks to provide a bottled tea that tastes like tea –a world of flavor, freshly brewed, and barely sweetened. We seek to provide better tasting, healthier teas the way nature and their cultures of origin intended them to be. We strive for relationships with our customers, employees, suppliers, and stakeholders that are as healthy and honest as the tea we brew.

Please note that this statement—the essential brand story—was written before a dime of start-up investment had been procured. It was written before a final product formula, packaging, labeling or plans for manufacturing and distribution were developed. It is written in plain, active language with no trite business clichés or obfuscations. And it says nothing about profit forecasts or growth projections. That's why I call it a guiding beacon. If the beacon shines brightly enough with authenticity, tenacity and perseverance, it can lead to the successful execution of its promise.

If you ever face writing a mission, remember that it is the alchemy of all you wish for. Great business alchemists always deal with feelings as much as facts. The Honest Tea business plan is full of what makes the brand a human invention rather than a purely rational spreadsheet of attributes and financials. It is written as a quest to inspire both those in and outside the company, and you don't do that by showing them your bank statement.

ONE STEP AT A TIME

If you have ever dreamed of building a consumer products company from scratch, you will find *Mission In A Bottle* to be an inspirational how-to manual. This includes what you are likely to encounter in the form of heartaches and heart warmth, agonies and ecstasies, and all manner of dogged determination through false starts and dead ends to eventual victory.

Before long, within a few weeks actually, the brand had its first bottle supplier, some preliminary recipes cooked up in Seth's kitchen with spring water, some organic cane sugar, honey, maple syrup and spices. A label design was in the works through another of Barry's students at Yale, and Seth found somebody who had worked in the start-up of several health foods to help them identify a supplier who could brew the tea in big enough batches.

RAISING THE MONEY

Meanwhile, Barry came up with a unique way of raising startup funds with warrants. Instead of the usual pretending a new enterprise could be worth some projected, made-up amount, Barry thought the level of success would determine what percentage of the company investors get for their money. The usual way is to assign a value of, let's say, a million dollars. Investors get 20 percent for their million while the founders keep 80 percent. Barry's scheme showed how he and Seth put investors' interests first as a token of thanks and trust. I'm not a financial guy, so bear with me as I attempt to explain it.

Barry proposed to give their start-up investors 100 percent of the company right off the bat! He and Seth would share in the gains *only after they doubled the investors' money.* In other words, their first batch of options had an exercise price that was double the initial share price. As the company grew in value, Seth and Barry would also gain, but only after the stock price doubled in value. As the enterprise appreciated in value, the partners would benefit proportionately through the stock warrants. Since they didn't have any shares to vote, they also had to get the investors to give them control for the first ten years. Through Barry's network of connections, investors ate this scheme up. Or should I say, drank it up. They sold 1.24 million shares at 50 cents and had what is known as warrants with exercise prices at $1 (100 percent return), $1.50 (200 percent return), $2.50 (400 percent return), $5

(900 percent), and $7.50 (1,400 percent). It shows that creative thinking is not reserved for poets and musicians, and that leadership can take many forms that work best when seen to be in everybody's best interest rather than one-sided and greedy.

THE JOURNEY

Getting a good idea like Honest Tea is one thing. Making it happen in real life is quite another. It involves costing ingredients, formulas that offer different flavors for different tastes, manufacturing, packaging, transport and marketing against formidable competition from established brands managed by experienced people not thrilled to see your arrival on their turf. The partners knew very little about the bottled drink category, but Barry used his knowledge of economics and innovation to come up with financial projections that would work in both trade and the consumer market place. Seth's personal energy and ability to connect with people did its part with all the sales and logistics. None of its early gestation suggests that Honest Tea came on the scene in the blaze of glory of a David up against Goliath, but against all odds, ten years after the brand took its first breaths and learning from mistakes made along the way, success eventually attracted a new partner in the form of Coca Cola, which bought 40 percent of the company for $43 million in 2008! Since then, Seth has stayed on as Tea-EO, while Barry has taken a less active role.

SOME THINGS NEVER CHANGE

I got to know Seth when he engaged my company, Brandtrust, to conduct in-depth research to discover the important touchpoints of Honest Tea consumers' understanding and motivation. As we have done for many brands, the point of our research was to use our unique deep-dive process to uncover the sweet spot of what consumers feel about the Honest Tea experience.

Says Seth, "We have only ever been interested in doing things with the dedication and commitment you might find in a nonprofit. Our approach has always aimed at caloric reduction in the American diet along with promotion of organic agriculture and fair trade labor standards. We want to connect people to the natural world through a beverage. In doing so, we took on the established way of doing things and won against all those who told us what we have to offer is not what consumers want. We did this with a certain naivety, so to make it a commercial success is a big thing I want to keep on doing. As Barry likes to say, 'We want to disprove H. L. Mencken's theory that nobody ever went broke underestimating the intelligence of the American public.'"

By sticking to its principles without any kind of compromise, the brand successfully came to occupy a unique "purple cow" space in the consumers' minds. Research shows that of all its many attributes, the one that stands out is an association with the word "honesty." In a veritable sea of dubious health claims, Honest Tea commands a distinct authenticity for one very simple reason: the brand delivers on its promise of great ingredients brewed with artisanal care in a drink that is thought to be healthy to begin with.

This perception is helped by the fact that drinking tea is considered to be more than a thirst-quenching break. It has a strong social component that any British person will recognize as true. At the first sign of a problem or call for a celebration, a Brit will "put the kettle on for a nice cuppa."

I've heard it said that the British army would never have been as successful in World War II if it had not been for the frequent tea breaks, and the Battle of Britain over the skies of England between the Royal Air Force and the German Luftwaffe during the early stages of that war might have failed without the comfort of "a nice hot cuppa Rosy Lee" (which is cockney rhyming slang for the word tea) awaiting the returning pilots on airfields all over the country.

Americans view tea-drinking a little differently, but some of the elements remain. I will be interested to see how well Starbucks does with its new Teavana venture. This can only be a sign of the beverage's growing popularity. With his customary vision, CEO Howard Shultz brought a fine-coffee sensibility to American social life. Since he does not do anything by half measure, I can only believe that when aided and abetted by Starbucks marketing determination, he might well do the same thing for tea. I see this as helping rather than poaching on the Honest Tea cause.

NO CONFLICT

One of the questions Seth is often asked is this: does selling your health-drink company to multi-national Coca Cola compromise your dedication to organic products, environmental quality and social justice? Here's how he answered one such query from a concerned young customer:

"Dear Julie,

Thanks for your honest opinion. Based on your remarks I think it's fair to say that you believe the world would be better if Coke sold more products like ours. So then the question is whether we believe Honest Tea will be corrupted by Coke. I'm confident we will continue to sell the products we've been selling. We painstakingly built our business over ten years in a very deliberate manner. We were constantly presented with the option of making products cheaper (e.g., using high-fructose corn syrup instead of organic cane sugar or honey, or tea leaves without fair trade certification) or with more calories, but we consistently chose to keep the brand "honest." Coke found value in what we have created. If they had wanted to change us into a company like theirs, they would have built their own brand rather than investing in Honest Tea. I hope you will judge us by our actions. Let me know if you see us backing away from our commitment to organics, healthier products and sustainability.

Honestly yours, Seth."

My own take on this is that the Coca-Cola Company is a very good marketer. Coke will want to see the Honest Tea brand perpetuate its success and has the funds and marketing clout to sustain brand extensions such as Honest Kids, which are healthy beverages kids seem to love. Great marketers know a good thing when they see one, and Honest Tea simply helps to extend Coke's reach in the marketplace with a very good and profitable consumer option. Coke will need no convincing to stick with the success of Honest Tea's quest.

KEEPING THE FIRE STOKED

As in all contemporary companies, employees become the lynchpins in keeping the brand on track for success by embracing and celebrating the brand's role in people's lives. Honest Tea's people share Seth's passion for the brand's social mission and its difference from other popular beverages. As Seth told me, "Employees who believe in what they do are more passionate, harder working and more loyal because they feel they are working for more than a paycheck. Ensuring the lasting value of these feelings comes about by the little things a company does that helps keep them engaged."

Once again we see a "heroic cause" at work. The brand's most recent mission has changed only slightly in the wording from over the years. It reads:

> *"Honest Tea seeks to create and promote great tasting, truly healthy organic beverages and we strive to grow our business with the same honesty and integrity we use to create our products with sustainability and great tea taste for all."*

To foster a sense of ownership, employees get their own budget to work with. Seth gives them the tools to manage their parts of the business, which fosters a real sense of trust and personal contribution.

Three times a year sales people get together to share experiences, compare notes for improvement and to have a bit of social fun. Managers go into regions to help launch a new distributor channel or a new retail account. They share inspiration and partner for joint promotions with other organic companies such as Stonyfield Farm. A collegial spirit of helping others prevails as a way to weld forces and inspire new ideas.

Distributors and retail customers are as important to the success of Honest Tea as the end user, which is why Honest Tea people do a lot of their work on site to help their retailers sell. This commitment builds trust where it counts—on the front lines. And every employee, including company accountants, goes on sales calls at least once a year. It's a small reminder that college degrees don't sell, people do, which is why many of the company's top sales people never graduated from college. Says Seth, "It's very easy to put together an impressive spreadsheet of tabs that display where sales come from, but reality comes from people, not spreadsheets."

MINE, ALL MINE

One thing I love is how individual employees are authorized to use the numbers under the UPC bar codes on the label for special recognition. The labeling code on the bottle is always expressed in eleven numbers, the last five of which are discretionary. An individual employee can use these numbers to recognize a special date, like a birthday. Last digits expressed as 6463 on a label could be the birth date of a family member born on June 4, 1963. The employee who uses it can take a bottle of tea home to show the family that she owns it! It's a little thing, and there's no charge for that, but the emotional return is priceless.

The company puts its money where its beliefs live when it comes to feeling strongly about promoting health. Wellness coaches are available to any employee who wants to follow a healthier lifestyle with diet and exercise—not a big thing in its own right, but one that shows employees how much the brand has their well-being at heart.

HOW HONEST ARE YOU?

Honesty is the brand's essential story. Seth always looks for ways to put it to work. He looks for ways to touch people in a personal way with the brand's story. He and his people go to fairs and festivals and set up Honest Tea booths so customers can sample the product and hear the brand story very directly, but one way he does this is with a truly remarkable social experiment he calls the National Honesty Index.

Says Seth, "We have this honest and transparent connection with our ingredients, so creating an activation that challenges consumers to think about these same values in the way they live makes sense."

The idea is to set up booths offering the product on the honor system. When you take a bottle of Honest Tea, you deposit one dollar. A custom mobile app is set up to record who stole and who paid. For the past five years, this social experiment has been staged over the course of ten days in more than sixty-one locations throughout all fifty states.

REFRESHING RESULTS

The findings are both amusing and encouraging with 91 percent of the 1,100 participants proving their honesty in 2013. Within the mix, citizens of Alabama and Hawaii proved to be most honest at 100 percent. Curiously, blondes turn out to be more honest than brunettes or redheads.

One man in South Carolina who did not pay felt guilty and later sent $2. Another not only stole a lot of product, but also tried to steal the cooler. And in the irony of ironies, in one location Seth got his bicycle stolen during the experiment!

I have never encountered a more imaginative way to connect with an audience to communicate the soul of a brand. Honest Tea proves once again that brands pursuing universal values with a heroic quest are by far the most successful for employees, consumers and shareholders alike. Hard evidence in many of the Fortune 500 companies proves this time and time again: brands with social purpose inspire a high level of engagement with all stakeholders, which makes them more profitable than brands that simply present a product benefit in a TV commercial and hope for the best. We all love and support people intent on doing the right thing and are attracted to what they have to offer.

HATS OFF

I raise a glass to Seth and Barry for their remarkable success—not by pulling the cork on a fine French wine, but by pouring a vintage of another color: Honest Tea's Peach Oo-la-long.

Here's to your good health, fellas. Let's all drink to that.

LESSON LEARNED—IT PAYS TO BE HONEST

There was a time not so long ago when companies could get away with misplaced, self-serving motives without getting caught. Many companies still try, but people can smell a rat a mile away and warn millions of other customers with a few keystrokes. Customers have too much experience and too many options to put up with anything that smacks of hyperbole or feels inauthentic. Trust me, it's not just that you're telling the truth, it's whether or not you are *actually* doing it. You cannot fake it. If your brand is not authentic, customers will know.

We're discovering that new brands and old brands seeking revival are much stronger when we think of them as causes or quests rather than businesses. When a company has an authentic higher-order reason to exist, the brand becomes that much more believable and appealing to customers. Higher order can be something you hope will change the world, like healthy organic beverages or something a bit more basic such as extraordinary customer service. Precisely what your company's higher order is matters less than whether or not it's real.

Why is honesty the best policy? Honest companies on a quest will not overlook or sidestep what matters most to customers. Creating valuable products and meaningful customer experiences is essential to their very nature. Your company becomes attractive to customers and they grow very loyal to your brands. And, if you're lucky, maybe even a world-class marketer such as the Coca-Cola Company will like your brand and what it stands for so much that they will buy it.

CHAPTER 8

Profit is Not a Dirty Four-Letter Word

I AM OFTEN ACCUSED OF BEING UTOPIAN WHEN I DISCUSS THE growing trend of brands adopting a social purpose as a potent marketing tool. One correspondent expressed his mistrust this way: "I am not a fan of brands having a 'higher calling.' It is altogether too presumptuous, arrogant and close to messianic. These are, after all, just companies, products and services, not a new religion or a life creed. I also think that they set themselves up for moral failure rather than delivering themselves from it."

This very common point of view is held by people who mysteriously equate profit with exploitation, but I see it more as the expression of incredulity that commerce can serve any kind of higher purpose beyond doing well by shareholders with the delivery of a cold-blooded return on their investment. In the harsh light of banking excesses in 2008 that apparently continue to this day with fraudulent Madoff-style investment advisers and sundry naughty corporate shenanigans, it's a very understandable position. One cynic's comment I read a couple of years ago is that banks are not too big to fail; they are too big to jail!

Psychologists tell us we have an innate capacity for deceit and that it is a survival skill we use to appear better than we are or to avoid punishment. The "little white lie" is a good example. It's something we all resort to, either to protect ourselves or to spare the feelings of a fellow human. It's a kind of camouflage like the lizard that changes color to avoid detection. It's mostly pretty harmless stuff until it becomes either a big fat harmful lie or against the law. Both people and brands do well to avoid even the harmless variety. Just as we have an instinctive ability to deceive, so do we also have an instinctive ability to smell out any kind of prevarication. If you did indeed cut down the cherry tree, do as George Washington is purported to have done: have the moral guts to fess up.

NOW FOR THE GOOD NEWS

Despite all the bad news out there, I see reason to believe that my correspondent might well be wrong on several counts of his doubt. Brands in the real world very often do create what he calls messianic followings. Think of how Harley Davidson riders flourish as a kind of tribe in their fierce pride of possession and how the brand lends its riders a collective social identity. And brands in the real world are often conceived to better the lives of their users and make a difference in the world at large. What blogger Joe Barnes wrote in a piece called "How to Succeed In Business Without Really Trying" might well be right: "Dislike and distrust doesn't stem from the pursuit of profit; rather, is comes from the pursuit of profit over doing what's right."

If you suddenly took away my washer and drier and my favored detergent, my life would become a lot more difficult. The inventors of these products must have seen that making life easier for busy people would be a powerful incentive. Ask Southwest's frequent flyer customers if any other profitable airline can come even close to matching its magic combination of caring, affordable, willing service. It's easy for me to believe that the folks who invented Tylenol wanted to relieve my headache without upsetting my stomach as a valuable contribution to a comfort I would be willing to pay for. Do these brands make money? You betcha. Was the attraction of big profit the deciding factor in the final decision to manufacture the products? Probably. And so what?

THE INVISIBLE HAND

The father of economics, Adam Smith, taught us way back in the 18th century that rational self-interest and competition lead to prosperity. The "invisible hand" of the marketplace works to promote the general good.

A venture capitalist might be interested to share in your desire to "change the world," but he or she will participate only if your revolutionary idea makes a big contribution to the lives of a lot of people who are willing to pay for and, therefore, make him or her big money. The motive to do good *and* make gobs of the stuff are not mutually exclusive. One feeds the other like a symbiotic relationship in nature.

The fact is, brands simply do not work in isolation from our lives. In the search for their own prosperity, they very often become the artifacts of our public and private identity in astonishing ways that speak to who and what we aspire to be, and this is what makes them profitable for the long run. People think of themselves as Apple guys, Chevy guys, Armani guys, etc. Harley guys don't like to be confused with Suzuki guys. It's the same for employees. For example, Cognex people proudly characterize themselves as Cognoids. They wouldn't do that if it did not enhance their self-perception. A company is just an article of incorporation, and a brand is more than a profit and loss statement. You have to think of a brand as flesh and blood, heart and soul, mind more than matter, feelings more than facts. This is why brands attract or repel us, or leave us indifferent. This is why we choose to adopt or reject or ignore them, and surely it all has a lot to do with our perception of their values, not just their utility. In this light, seeing a brand as a force for good in the world is as much an attribute as any practical benefit. And surely a culture of good values breeds the most coveted and profitable benefit of all: trust.

WATCH YOUR LANGUAGE

Perhaps it's the words. Moral purpose, heroic cause, social ideal and altruism are words not to be feared, but they may strike some as a bit high falutin'. They maybe turn off naysayers as too fancy, or as my correspondent says, too presumptuous. That's why my favorite word to define the pursuit of authentic brand values and extraordinary customer experiences is *quest*. I borrow it from Ty Montague's book *True Story: How To Combine Story and Action to Transform Your Business*. In his use of the word, it means the contribution your brand makes in its driving ambition. I like it because it signifies something important in the form of action. It suggests an experience, an adventure, a never-ending journey. As Ty points out, it is the word for companies that *do* stories rather than *tell* them. Companies that are story doers rather than storytellers become successful because they represent stories told primarily through actions and experiences, not advertising. People literally adopt them and take them to heart because they portray authentic values and experiences that contribute to their users lives in unique ways. These are brands you join rather than simply use. As Ty says, "Story-doing companies don't just practice what they preach – they actually preach *by* practicing.

NOT EXACTLY "JACK AND JILL"

We're not talking narratives here like "Jack and Jill went up the hill ..." or the message we get from a commercial like, "Heinz ketchup is too thick, too rich to run." These are good stories we are *told*. But as Ty writes, "Metastory is a story that is *told through action.* It is not a story that you *say*, it's a story that you *do*. Every individual has one. You have one. And every company has one, too." Connect story doing to the word "quest" and you see that a company like Southwest gives us many concrete examples of what is meant by story doing. We will be talking a lot more about story-doing quests as we go along.

When you think about what traits a brand could ideally adopt in the pursuit of common good and the generation of loyalty, the word "quest" works pretty well, and at the same time it lacks the possible stigma of too-intense do-goodism. An old-school businessperson might better understand and take to the word quest rather than brand ideal, heroic cause, social purpose, etc.

THE HEART OF THE MATTER

When I say that profit comes to those who most abundantly offer us a societal reason for being in the form of a quest, I do not imply that seeking profit from simple performance is in any way *anti*social. There are many categories full of workmanlike, utilitarian brands. If you like eggs because they are tasty, easy to prepare and relatively inexpensive, that's fine, and most any basic brand in the supermarket will do. That is, until someone convinces you of their quest that free-range eggs are healthier, taste better and are better for the chickens that so generously lay them. They share the story of how and why their organic, free-range eggs are better, and they create an experience for you to taste their eggs. Once you experience the brighter yellow yolks and taste the richer flavor, you agree the eggs are better. You want to be part of something good and true because it makes you feel better about yourself and your efforts to become a better and healthier person, mother, wife, etc. You join the quest, and that particular brand of eggs that you happily pay more for becomes your brand of choice. Until you knew there was a reason for it, you probably don't give a hoot about its quest.

Salt is a perfect example. Morton is my salt and I refuse to buy any other brand even though it costs about thirty percent more than other brands. It's silly, but if my market is out of Morton, I go to another store or put off buying salt until it is available. I tell myself, "It's just salt." Technically speaking, salt is salt—just simple molecules of sodium chloride. It truly is the perfect example of a commodity since every brand by necessity is made from identical molecules.

It makes no sense that I won't even consider another brand. But I have positive memories of Morton that make me feel good. My mother uses the brand exclusively; I've never seen another brand in her cupboard or on her table. Each time I reached for salt during a family dinner, every time my food needed more flavor, Morton met my needs. Yes, any other brand works fine, but Morton now occupies a permanently positive place in my brain even though, for decades now, the company has spent very little on advertising. Still, I know the Morton slogan, "When it rains it pours." It's a very basic quest, but the company has been on it since 1911 when apparently salt did not flow so freely.

It has certainly served them well. Morton Salt consistently maintains about a 50 percent share of the market in the United States. During consumer research, participants were told a competitive store brand was the exact same product, even packaged by Morton, and many chose

Morton nonetheless. Apparently, the brand makes them feel better, too. I know it makes me feel good that so many other people share my irrational preference for Morton Salt. This should also make every senior executive—even those in commodity businesses—feel better realizing it is possible that their brands can overcome "me too" brand status and command higher and more profitable margins. Seriously, if it can be done with salt, it can be done with any product.

The pursuit of an authentic quest is the surest way to generate greater loyalty, success and profit. No company can survive (let alone prosper) without a healthy profit any more than we who work for wages to put bread on our tables can survive recurring negative numbers at the bottom of our tax returns. Even non-profits cannot survive without the generous souls who donate to their causes. By the same token, both not-for-profit and for-profit organizations only get revenue in accordance with how well they deliver whatever we determine to be their emotional value. In the end, brands only prosper or fail based on how we feel about them. A brand that offers an authentic experience of practical *and* social value is surely more attractive than one that is simply practical. If you drive a Toyota Prius, you're getting good wheels plus the good feeling of spewing less pollution.

A REASON FOR BEING

The reality remains a simple fact: if a brand performs as expected but also gives us a reason to buy it beyond its utility, it stands that it is more likely to find a spot in our shopping basket and a coveted crease in the emotional parts of our brain. It appears that doing good and doing well can indeed be part and parcel of the motive for growth and higher profit, and more companies see the financial and psychological advantages of pursing this very course.

This much seems obvious to me: a quest that involves a social purpose or heroic cause must automatically involve intrinsic, ongoing touchpoints in the experience of the brand that can significantly influence purchase and long-term loyalty. Surely this is the healthiest foundation for the phenomenon of profit.

Peter Drucker taught such a lesson to the Japanese after World War II when, as a country, it earned a well-deserved reputation for producing cheap goods, otherwise known as crap. In his most persuasive manner, this is what the venerable consultant told his Japanese business clients who widely took his advice to heart and gained the reputation they have for quality today:

"Making money is a necessity of survival. It is also the result of performance and a measurement of it, but making money is in itself not a performance. The purpose of a business is to create a customer and to satisfy a customer. That is performance and what the business is being paid for. The job and function of management as the leader, decision maker, and value setter of the organization, and indeed, the purpose and rationale for the organization altogether is to make human beings productive so the skills, expectations, and beliefs of the individual lead to achievement in joint performance."

I have used this quote so often that I remember it by heart. It never fails to raise the eyebrows of people who insist that financial performance is the one and only Holy Grail of a company's *raison d'etre*. But the question remains: does Drucker's position hold up in the super-competitive world of business today? The answer is that it holds up more than ever.

In a recent op-ed article in the New York Times, columnist David Brooks expressed it well when he said capitalism doesn't work as well as it can when it relies on the profit motive alone: "If everybody is just chasing material self-interest, the invisible hand won't lead to well-functioning markets. It will just lead to arrangements in which market insiders take advantage of everybody else. Capitalism requires the full range of what motivates, including the intrinsic drive for knowledge and fairness."

SHOW ME

In *Grow: How Ideals Power Growth and Profit At The World's Greatest Companies*, former P&G world-wide marketer Jim Stengel posits the argument that "maximum growth and high ideals are not incompatible. They're inseparable." The great business leaders of today, every man and woman profiled in this book, would heartily agree.

Jim's argument refines Drucker's and Brook's ideas and brings them up to date with practical evidence that "doing the right thing" is good for a company's financial value, that the most productive way of doing business nowadays is based on improving the lives of people the business serves, and it is rooted in the timeless fundamentals of business and human nature. He maintains that a brand ideal is a business's reason for being because it's the only sustainable way to recruit, unite and inspire all the people a business touches, including both employees and customers. He makes enormous sense to me, particularly since it comes from a guy who, as one of the top honchos in a package-goods marketing juggernaut, did a growth study of more than 50,000 brands around the world to validate his findings and narrowed them all down to what he calls The Stengel Top Fifty.

Writes Jim, "By operating according to the principles in this framework, the world's best businesses achieve growth three times or more than that of the competition in their categories ... If you want great business results, you and your brand have to stand for something compelling. And that's where brand ideals enter the equation."

This means that the usual way of exploiting a practical brand advantage with what we used to call a Unique Selling Proposition expressed in repetitive, one-way advertising messaging no longer cuts enough mustard. Our customers want more in the form of a brand they can trust to do right by them beyond product claims, and more and more employees are adopting similar attitudes. In an age of instant communication, what a brand stands for matters just as much as what a brand says or does. It's not that advertising doesn't work. It still does. But with heightened customer power in the new digital age, it's not enough. It's the *peak experiences* of the brand that really count. That's why Amazon CEO Jeff Bezos took all funds allocated to advertising and put them into perfecting customer service he knew would create brand ambassadors that are more effective with positive word-of-mouth than advertising messaging. Improving customer service as an ongoing quest means improving the critical touchpoints from the beginning to the end of the customers' experience of the brand. It's why quests that excite and involve both inside and outside the company provide the modus operandi for start-ups who can't afford hundred-million dollar advertising budgets to get their story out there, but instead count on their customers to tell and spread their stories for them. Zappos is another brand that does very little advertising. They prefer to put their money toward improving the experience as a better form of generating big buzz. People consistently share how much they love, love, love the Zappos experience, and Amazon is on the top of the best customer services companies year in and year out.

Going further, what if a company tied all of its functions to its metastory? What if its metastory defined its growth strategy? What if there were no internal silos, but every department and all functions and customer touchpoints were organized around the metastory? Ty Montague: "That would be a company designed so that every action in every department helped to advance the story, every product had the story baked into it, and every customer interaction would be designed to create the maximum amount of meaning in the hearts and minds of customers. A company like that would be extremely efficient. And it would be very hard to beat by competitors who were still structured for the previous age."

This is what I mean when I say a brand's focus and energy are best guided by a handful of critical experiences that matter most and can be discovered with careful investigation. You do not have to get everything right any more than you will ever gain 100 percent perfection. Stuff does and will happen along the path of a customer's experience with your brand. But mistakes and omissions are best forgiven or simply overlooked when you get the critical touchpoints leading to peak experience right.

Many companies still have a long way to go to fully get the hang of presenting their customers with anything more than a practical product benefit promoted through advertising, but Jim Stengel, Ty Montagu (and hopefully I) give you more than enough examples to show that there is indeed a wee glimmer at the end of that old tunnel. It is a fortunate fact that people universally love to hitch their wagon to a cause and a quest that is bigger than themselves. This includes people who manage brands and inspire their staffs. The companies featured in this book are witness to the phenomenon.

THE MAGIC OF THE BUSINESS ARTISTS

Jim's own study of the ten-year performance of the top fifty brands in twenty-eight categories began by asking three critical questions: Are the bonds that people form with brands the ultimate growth driver? If so, what kind of bond generates the most growth? And how can business leverage it? I love the simple clarity of these questions for getting to the root of what an ideal cause can (or cannot) mean practically.

He discovered that brand ideals drive the performance of the highest growth businesses under the guidance of "business artists" who excel with very similar practices covering five fields of fundamental human values. For example, some like Coca Cola *elicit joy*. Some like FedEx and Starbucks *enable connection*. Some like Amazon and Apple *inspire exploration.* Some like Jack Daniels and Mercedes-Benz *evoke pride.* And others like Stonyfield Farm *impact society.*

Jim gives us detailed case histories in *Grow* that are as readable as detective stories, and a Harvard Business Review story (September 2013) backs his claims with examples of how many major companies go about implementing social purpose on behalf of their brands in ways that generate good will and exemplary profit.

A quest by its very definition will not inspire your customers if it is limited to "making money." Getting personally rich might understandably turn your crank, but you making tons of money does nothing for the people you are trying to attract, involve and excite, and that above all is what a business is supposed to do.

EXAMPLES GALORE

Nestle, Unilever and Danone are working to reposition themselves as nutrition and health companies. To this end, Danone even sold off its beer, meat and cheese units while it acquired other dairy products along with water, baby food and medical nutrition businesses.

Carmakers Nissan and Toyota are redefining their purpose with low emission vehicles. IBM's "Let's make a smarter planet" is the expression of its quest to improve education and health care. Dow exploits its tradition of innovation to make canola and sunflower seeds that produce oils with lower levels of saturated fat and no trans fats. CVS Pharmacies are on a quest to play a more active, supportive role in each person's unique health experience—including a very public and positive decision to eliminate tobacco products from their stores. And Becton Dickenson developed the world's first syringe to protect health workers from needle-stick injuries that can cause HIV and other infections. This last initiative turned into a $2 billion dollar business that accounts for 25 percent of the company's revenue.

The list goes on with Nestle helping millions of malnourished families in India to get inexpensive micronutrient-reinforced spices, thus creating a profit opportunity in the bargain. GE partners in a social enterprise with Embrace to distribute a $200 incubator for keeping infants that were prematurely born alive in India. And Zappos took an online shoe company to a $2 billion business within ten years by selling, of all things, the quest for happiness.

It's all wonderful stuff that feeds the notion that one does not need to carry placards in the streets to pursue the quest of an ideal cause; in fact, looking at ways your company can improve its social enterprise with small initiatives that cost little or nothing can be a good place to start a revolution in your organization. As Jim Stengel says, "Remain stuck inside your current business model, and your business days are numbered. Make a brand ideal your North Star and the sky's the limit." Not to be overlooked is what a brand ideal in the form of a quest can do to motivate employees with a higher sense of purpose and commitment to an inspiring vision.

It's just plain magical.

INSIGHT—THERE IS GREAT PROFIT IN A QUEST.

When businesses strive to do something better—reform an industry, streamline a process, right a wrong or simply treat customers well— they create such positive feelings and experiences that doing it better becomes the most important thing. When you focus on doing the right things, people, starting with employees, experience your integrity firsthand and naturally trust you more. Trust leads to loyalty, and people team up with you and join your cause. Nothing is more valuable or profitable to a company than loyalty.

The rewards for companies that get this are evident in their performance: tracked for fifteen years, the stock returns of the Forbes Top 100 Companies to Work For outperformed the S&P 500 and Russell 3000 nearly two to one.

It rarely costs more to do the right thing. People embrace brands that strive to meet a higher calling. Customers recognize the inherent value of a quest for better products and services. Employees are motivated to be a part of something meaningful. Because there's no charge for being a true champion, we see through the real stories in this book that doing the right thing, the human thing, is also highly profitable.

CHAPTER 9

How to Find a Relevant Quest

ONE OF MY RULING MANTRAS IS THIS: IF YOU REALLY NEED TO
know why people do what they do, the worst thing you can do is
ask them.

I see this as an abiding truth for the simple reason most of us cannot
(or will not) articulate our innermost emotions even to ourselves. You
have to get below the conscious surface the way a miner has to dig
to discover the riches of ore. When you do it right, you might even
find gold.

This is one of the guiding principles of my team at Brandtrust in
our quest to help companies deeply understand their customers to get
at what brands really do for them beyond mere utility. Our research
techniques based on social psychology and behavioral economics
very effectively draw out the most important, often unarticulated,
emotions and motivations associated with a specific brand's meaning.
Our visualization, narrative pattern recognition and ethnographic
observation techniques elicit the most resonant stories about how the
brand's relevance is created through just a handful of experiences. The
insights derived from these research methods are invaluable for leading
established companies to the discovery of their unique metastories and
relevant quests.

A good example: Danaher, the maker of Craftsmen hand tools for
Sears, asked my team to find out why customers are so loyal to the
Craftsman brand. We discovered motivations that were beyond anything

we as brand researchers and consultants ever thought possible—namely, that tools are much more than devices to fix things. They represent a fascinating rite of passage on the part of men who grew up watching their role models work with tools. Boys live for the moment when they are asked to help. Tools apparently represent strength, reliability and power. Men strive to emulate the masculine characteristics embodied by their tools. These insights encouraged Craftsman to position their hand tools to the key emotional drivers of confidence, pride and honor. These revelations helped Danaher understand the relevance of specific retail experiences that helps Craftsman to continue holding a commanding share of the market. The insights also explain why most men love hardware stores as symbols of their most masculine selves even when they don't know one end of a hammer from the other!

JACK LOVES JILLS

One of our research techniques, Emotional Inquiry™, helped Jack Daniels to understand the unspoken drivers of female trial, preferences and loyalty. Surprisingly, in a social context, masculinity is apparently not the best way to describe what Jack Daniels means to people; in fact, "empowering" is a more accurate word to describe what men *and* women alike truly feel about the brand. The social context of Jack Daniels suggests that it can be gender neutral. To a woman "empowerment" represents the connection between the brand Jack Daniels and her true self—her confidence, independence and empowered femininity. These rather surprising insights provided a means to attract women to the brand without changing the brand's iconic essence.

We do not know what we might be missing without very close encounters with a brand's deep-seated reason for being. A brand's real social meaning is mostly opaque to conscious scrutiny. As already noted, it is not easily articulated because, like much of human motivation, it lives far below any kind of conscious level.

SNORKELING DOESN'T CUT IT.

You need to shift your mental mode from "voice of customer" to "mind of customer" to understand what's really going on in their heads. As much as modern social science finds Freudian theory full of holes, it was good old Sigmund who woke us up to the reality that we have far less access to what goes on in our brains than we like to believe. This is why traditional focus groups and surveys have limited utility. They can tell you *what* people do but not *why*. They can give you *rationalizations* but not the real motivational drivers. To get that, you can't just snorkel. You have you go deep into people's memories to expose what is really behind their beliefs and behaviors. A psychiatrist conducting group therapy, for example, is not going to get the same results as one who affords a patient the sanctity of private evaluation.

The reality of how we process information can even affect how we approach the logic of solving problems. When we helped the Centers for Disease Control and Prevention tackle the problem of second-hand smoke, conventional wisdom might have led to attacking smokers as evil monsters out to do harm, which would have been highly offensive and probably ineffective. Our findings led to a different approach that might never have been discovered with the superficial findings you get from surveys or focus groups. The solution was to motivate non-smokers to form a huge lobbying group that inspired government to take the actions that make public places as smoke-free as they are today. If you smoke and hate it when you have to go outside in freezing weather to light up, you now know whom to blame! You will find this and many other examples in our last book, *How does it Make You Feel: Why Emotion Wins The Battle of the Brands.*

THE WIRED CONCLUSION

It turns out that quests for the common good are by no means unnatural or extraordinary. Behavioral scientists are actually beginning to understand altruism as a neural mechanism. The small kindnesses and incidents of caring brands I talk about in this book go well with the theory that the drive for social connection is equally as strong as self-interest. In many ways they are one in the same. As Mathew D. Lieberman puts it in *Why Our Brains Are Wired To Connect*, "In addition to self-interest we are also interested in the welfare of others. This, along with self-interest, is part of our basic wiring."

If you think of "customer satisfaction" as a process of collaboration between you and your customers for its achievement, it also stands to reason that a genuine desire to do right by them in ways that go beyond a simple commercial transaction works to the benefit of all and could be considered as an essential brand attribute. It's what loyalty is made of, including the loyalty born from the depth of your relationship with your employees.

For customers and employees alike, you can do a lot worse than to run your business on the advice of Mark Twain, who said, "Always do right. It will gratify some people and astonish the rest.". And another clue to the wisdom of a shared purpose is found in the meaning of the word "company,": originally defined by the French as "the sharing of bread.".

A DEFINITION

If you see the benefit of an ideal-centered quest in your company's profit ambitions, I can think of no better motivation than Jim Stengel's definition of what the words mean in that context:

1. The key to unlock the code of business for 21st century business success.

2. The only sustainable way to recruit, unite, and motivate all the people a brand touches, from employees to customers.
3. The most powerful lever a business can use to achieve competitive advantage.
4. A business's essential reason for being.
5. The factor connecting the core beliefs of the people inside the business with the fundamental human values of the people they serve.
6. Not social responsibility or altruism, but a program for profit and growth based on improving people's lives.

LESSON LEARNED—QUESTS ARE BORN FROM EMPATHY

A.G. Lafley, Proctor & Gamble's , CEO, makes the case for empathy abundantly clear in his book *The Game Changer.* It requires deep understanding of what drives the consumers' *emotions.* It requires understanding not only their need, but, also their *aspirations.* You must get an appreciation for who they are, how they live, and—yes, of course—how your product can best improve their lives.

Just put yourself in you customer's shoes and truly strive to understand how you can improve their emotional well-being with your products and services. Your quest can be crazy complicated or stunningly simple depending on what is determined as a wrong to right, a problem to solve or paradigm to shift. You can have a big, hairy, audacious quest to change the world, or simply aspire to make your customer's experience the best it can be. It doesn't matter how grand or how basic your cause is, as long as you actually have one.

CHAPTER 10

An Extraordinary Leader.
Extraordinary Results.

I'VE MET HUNDREDS OF IMPRESSIVE EXECUTIVES IN THE COURSE
of my working life, but none more so than Tom Feeney.

Spend fifteen 15 minutes with him and you come away wanting
to take on the world. "Dynamic" does do not do him justice, and it all
seems to come from him as naturally as breathing. No bombast. No
chest thumping. Just good old plain enthusiasm, along with an obvious
concern for his people and the customers and clients they serve.

Tom is President and CEO of Safelite Group. When he came on board
in 1988, it was a conglomerate of dozens of regional brands involved
in windshield manufacturing and vehicle glass replacement. Tom led
the charge to put them all together, including new acquisitions, as one
national auto glass juggernaut called Safelite AutoGlass.

Within four of his five years as leader, he doubled the business and
took the company from $500 million to an awesome mind-boggling
worth of $1.2 billion. In tough economic times, he also tripled profits.
And he did it with a service that is as welcome in people's lives as a
root canal!

TAKING IT TO THE STREETS

One of the big transformative decisions was to get auto glass
replacement mostly out of the shop and take it directly to the customer's
home with a mobile service. This meant abandoning the old franchising
way of doing business to go with company-owned mobile centers. In

turn, this put the onus on having technicians with great customer-service skills, which required significant time investment in training for personal contact—not just one house call at a time, but as a never-ending commitment. One advantage to this business model was that it made big sense to the insurance companies that account for 50 percent of the replacement and repair business. To them it meant they could outsource their low-value auto glass claims to concentrate on more complicated cases like personal injury and home fires that require greater analytical skills. At the same time, it transformed the lives of the people who do the work.

PEOPLE FIRST

As we witness in so many service-dependent companies, it's difficult to see which comes first: care for employees or care for the customer. It becomes more and more obvious that you cannot achieve excellence in one without simultaneous excellence in the other, particularly if your mission is to become *the natural choice for vehicle glass repair and replacement services in the United States.* As Tom says, "Having great people is the ultimate competitive advantage. If your goal is to treat every customer as if they were your only customer, you need people with exemplary social skills in their DNA."

He adds that when you provide mobile service to customers as opposed to them coming to a fixed facility, you've actually raised the service bar. They don't give you the keys and sit in a waiting room. But if you pull into their driveway fifteen minutes later than the scheduled time, they aren't happy. Customer expectations are higher, and you must have systems and motivations in place to meet that expectation.

ONE AT A TIME ALL THE TIME

One thing that had to be abandoned was a strict productivity measurement. It's a metric that is important in many businesses: Get in and get out as quickly as possible and go on to the next customer. But with one-on-one service on the customer's turf, what Tom calls "qualitivity" matters more than productivity. This is particularly true when it comes to the health and well-being of something as important to you as your beloved automobile. When you tie compensation to productivity, you are actually encouraging the technician to get to the next job as fast as possible. Speed is still important, but it must never come at the expense of the interchange with the customer who quite naturally sees his windshield as the most important one you have to take care of that day.

When Tom switched to another method of tying performance to compensation, it had a great effect on the technicians and a corresponding rise in customer satisfaction. As Tom says, "These are craftsmen who enjoy working with tools. They have a natural desire to be proud of their work. When I told them, 'You will be more rewarded by our company when you can really take care of the customer you're dealing with than if you feel the need to rush off to the next one,' we really tapped into their pride in a job well done and a customer well taken care of. It also helped in our determination to put the customer at the center of everything we do. One way to do that was to let our technicians just be themselves."

The new initiative raised some skeptical eyebrows within the company from those who worried that productivity would suffer, but Tom is not easily deterred, and everybody now acknowledges that it has been one of the driving forces of the company's current success, a success that sees no horizon.

With that one action, he turned every one of his technicians into social and technical entrepreneurs. With time out of the equation, they were no longer just working for a paycheck. They were working for pride, for mastery of both the work to be done and the success of the relationship with the customer. It doesn't get any better than that. It's a classic case of just getting "management" out of the way and letting people do their thing!

TAKING THE HELM

The first stages of the new process took several years to put in place, but it accelerated rapidly when Tom became president and CEO in 2008. Before Tom, the company had been run mainly by operations, and as he says, operations executives march to a different drummer than service execs. One is process- and efficiency-oriented; the other is customer- and communications-oriented. Tom saw the latter as the real opportunity to take the company to a more profitable, more stimulating, more creative place for the employees that could not help but end up with larger numbers of happy customers willing to become advocates for the brand. If you define leadership as the ability to affect change, you define what makes Tom Feeney a truly great leader.

A GREAT LEADER CREATES ENGAGEMENT

When you decide to put people rather than process at the center of your ability to affect change, it helps if you actually like doing that! Tom does. He really likes getting out there to listen and exchange and look at different opinions. He says, "There are no filters between me and the customer or staff. There are four interruptions I will take in my day no matter what I'm doing: a call from a customer, a client, an employee or my wife. No exceptions."

He goes on to say, "We are a subsidiary of an international company called Belron. When I shared my position on interruptions with our global CEO, he said, 'What about me?' My answer was that he is not on the list. I will, of course, take his call, but it is not a priority like any of the others. I can always call him later, but I will not do that with a customer, a client or an employee if I can possibly help it."

TO ILLUMINATE, COMMUNICATE

You might be surprised if you call Safelite with a complaint and get put through to Tom. To him, complaints present an important opportunity for direct customer communication and must never be avoided by a manager. He says that in his forty years in business, he can think of only three or four times he was not able to convert a disgruntled customer into a brand ambassador (as I heard one stand-up comic say recently, "I turned her from disgruntled into gruntled," which is funny but begs the question "What's coming next?").

Tom always starts with, "What can we do for you? What is the problem? How can I help you?" He finds that people generally respond well when you ask these questions and mean them, and once again, solving one customer's problem can end up making her a brand advocate, which is the best form of advertising.

The principle of genuine concern applies equally well to employees. They need good tools to do their jobs well, and one of the best tools you can give them is trust that their company cares about what they think and have to say. This is the only way you can get them truly on board for more than money.

PEOPLE POWERED

In the toughest times of the 2008 recession, Tom fought the company-wide reflex to cut costs by spending a million-and-a-half dollars to bring 600 people to Orlando, Florida, so he could share with them his vision for the future.

In his words, "When a leader wants to initiate massive change he has to be able to look people in the eye and speak to them very directly. I told them. 'We cannot worry about all the bad stuff going on in the economy. We can only worry about what we can control. We call this 'controlling the controllables.' In order to transform this company for growth, we must first transform ourselves. Our future will be made very bright by moving from a 20th century operations company to this new century as a service company, which means investing in our people so that they understand the needs of our customers. We have to start looking at our business through the eyes of our customers, and we will do that now by putting our people first. People driven by the power of intention have a strong will that won't permit anything to interfere with achieving their goals. People powered, not policy powered, is how this company will deliver extraordinary service for extraordinary results. We will not aim for customer satisfaction. We will aim for customer delight!"

At the end of hearing this in our interview, I felt like asking him where can I sign up, but apparently not everybody was so readily brought on board. Safelite is basically a blue-collar business. It isn't Microsoft or Apple. It's in a negative services category, as in people hate it when they have to see you. But Tom figured that the craftsman's desire to do good work would only increase if he could show his technicians the way to encourage appreciation on the part of customers. And, of course, managers used to concentrating on efficient operations would have to also understand the subtleties of service.

As said in the lesson of an ancient Chinese proverb: "Tell me and I'll forget; show me and I may remember; involve me and I'll understand." Tom needed to involve them so that they could understand.

A STORY PAINTS A THOUSAND PICTURES

When Tom gets wind of a great service story on the part of a technician, he quickly recreates the action of it in a video and sends it company-wide. These stories get him very excited. He calls them "Greatness In Action." He told me one that clearly brought emotion to his voice:

Kanyon Hilliare is a technician who works in Portland, Oregon. He discovered that one of the customers he was called upon to serve was deaf. Every job starts with meeting the customer to explain exactly what needs to be done, and Kanyon did not want to skip this important point of contact. His solution was sheer genius at work.

He knew a friend who could do sign language. The night before the scheduled meeting with the customer, Kanyon went to the friend's house and shot a video on his smart phone. He had the friend stand next to him doing sign language while he verbally explained the process as he intended to do with the customer. When Tom learned of it, he immediately called Kanyon to ask him how he came up with the idea. Kanyon said, "It was just part of my job. There was an obstacle I had to overcome if I wanted to get it right."

Tom saw this as a perfect example of what we call "story do" rather than story tell. He got Kanyon and his friend together with a professional video maker and recreated the scene. He then sent the story to the entire Safelite world of 10,000 associates, including 4,500 technicians and forty-three field-based technical trainers in ninety-two markets led by district managers as an example of what outstanding service really means.

Tom says, "You can't teach stuff like that, but the example might create the inspiration to do better and better and better. It plays into the idea of getting results by looking at our business through the eyes of our customers, making it easy for them to do business with us and making sure their experience is memorable enough to tell their neighbors, friends and family how delightful it is to deal with people who care."

As a result of Kanyon's insight, the company recorded professional videos that technicians can access for all deaf and hard of hearing customers.

TALK TO ME

Tom has an AskTom email in which any employee can ask any question he or she wants, and Tom guarantees an answer within one week. If the person gives him permission, he then publishes it for everybody to see on the company intranet. If the person prefers to remain private, Tom asks if he can publish it anonymously. The only question he won't answer in print is one to do with an associate's pay. On that one, he gets back to them on the phone. He takes questions at home and will not let anybody feel that a question being asked is a silly one. And he makes anniversary calls. When he sends a letter, it is always with a handwritten note attached. He encourages his fellow managers to follow his example with rewards and awards for great service rendered. This guy is a communication dynamo. I hope every exec reading this chapter takes notes on how it is done.

Tom confirms the thesis that doing little things add up to big things that mean lot more than big words. He says, "I just do what I would like other people to do for me if I were in their shoes. It's not easy going out there and doing what these guys do. Hearing how much it's appreciated from their CEO personally is something I would have enjoyed. Come to think of it, I like hearing it from *my* CEO."

HOW DOES ANYBODY GET TO BE LIKE TOM?

Ask him his background and he will tell you he's a recovering accountant! He started as an auditor for Hertz before he became a city manager in the Palm Beach car rental division. Within three months on the job he gained seventeen market share points, which prompted a call from the CEO to ask him how in the world he did it.

Tom says, "It was basically instinctive. I simply studied the plane schedules and figured that when planes arrived there had to be customers on them. I got the garage attendants to work in the evening to get the cars ready so we wouldn't have to scramble in the morning and keep a customer waiting at the counter. I also sized up the competition and saw that they weren't coming to work until 10 A.M. I wondered if these guys were there to retire. That's how we took share from them. I loved feeling that rush when a customer is coming at you, and I never liked feeling the pain when you don't have a car ready for them. I've washed cars, gassed cars. I've worked with the garage attendants.

I believe you have to understand what they do so you can relate to them and help them do their best work. There are no menial jobs. Only menial attitudes."

A year later he was promoted to the Miami airport, which was the third-largest Hertz profit center in the world. Even on that much larger scale he grew share by six percentage points, which was substantial.

Said Tom, "They offered me a $500 raise. And I resigned. They flew a bunch of people down from New York to ask me why. I said, 'We've had great results and you're telling me there's a hold on payroll policy?' They offered me $10,000 to stay, which was much more than I actually wanted but I said, 'No. I've made my decision.' I think there's a lesson in leadership in there somewhere."

Today, Tom has maintained a strong relationship with Hertz and considers them a valuable key client. The moral of this story is people want to work for a lot more than money. They want to work for meaning and they want to work for results. Surely outstanding service to any cause must be properly recognized with financial as well as emotional reward.

AN ARTIST AT WORK

The problem with a guy like Tom is that you can never pay him enough for what he does. He is more than a businessman. He is a business artist. An artist gives us priceless gifts in the form of insight and new ways of seeing life. That's what Tom gives his people through decisive, daring initiatives and new ways of seeing work that liberate them from the feeling of simply being cogs in a corporate machine. He turns every one of his people into linchpins of self-directed entrepreneurship. And in doing this he also rewards himself in ways that have nothing to do with money. Tom is a giver. He gives of himself; therefore, he receives. There is a lesson in this equation for all of us.

I was sorry to see my conversation with him come to an end, but I am a richer man for having had it. Thank you, Tom.

LESSON LEARNED—"QUALITIVITY" MATTERS MORE THAN PRODUCTIVITY

We learn in business schools the notion that you can only manage what you can measure. It's a useful thought, but it tends to cause us to default to the things that are superficially easy to track. Time tracking is a perfect example. We've encountered many clients who still insist their customer service reps handle customer calls in a prescribed time period, usually as short as possible. The thinking is that the company doesn't make anything on those calls—they cost money. So turn them quicker and handle more calls at a lower overall cost. Yet, no one stops to consider the cost of lost customers from the poor service provided for those who can't resolve their problem in the allotted time. Or simply feel the service is dismissive. We've witnessed cases in which phone service reps actually hang up on customers when their two minutes run out. The reps are measured by time on the phone, not the customer's evaluation of the experience. Even if the reps aren't hanging up on them, the customers can sense the reps need to get off the phone. You know how that feels, don't you? You can tell. Customers can, too.

Consider the irony of this. Customer service representatives are the front line of your organization. They talk with thousands of customers every day, either building trust or endangering it. What could be more important? What could be a more worthwhile investment? Yet, customer service reps are often poorly-recruited, insufficiently-trained, low-paid workers who have little or no stature within the company. No wonder so many of them refer to themselves as "mushrooms—kept in the dark and fed you know what."

It's just as feasible to measure what matters most—customer experience and the loyalty built through those encounters. And, it's just as easy to engage employees to do what will delight customers and turn those metrics into values. I love Tom's phrase that "Qualitivity matters more than productivity," but the next time I talk with him, I may suggest he should alter it ever so slightly to state, "Qualitivity drives real productivity."

CHAPTER 11

Don't Just Tell Your Story, Do It

IN 1982, AN AUSTRIAN TOOTHPASTE COMPANY EXEC BY THE NAME of Dietrich Mateshitz was on a business trip to Thailand suffering from what turned out to be a very fortunate mega dose of jet lag that goes with that kind of travel from the west. I say fortunate because it led him to the discovery of an unusual cure that would bring something new to the world and make him super rich in the bargain.

What he found was a tonic called *Krating Daeng,* recommended by locals as an effective treatment that increased physical endurance and mental concentration. It will come as no surprise to many millions of us who have since tried this magic elixir in its western form as presented to us by Matetshitz that *Krating Dan* in English means "Red Bull."

The really surprising part of this story is that the man we could assume to be a conventional package goods salesman turned out to be (as Ty Montague says in *True Story: How to Combine Story and Action to Transform Your Business*) an extraordinarily talented storyteller and experiential marketer who had the immediate vision to see that Red Bull could become something far greater than another liquid in a can as it might have been treated by any of the big soft drink manufacturers. "From the beginning," says Ty, "Mateschitz viewed Red Bull as a lifestyle, a kind of belief system, a religion in which that can of liquid was necessary and functional."

In an article in *Fast Company* magazine, Mateschitz laid out his original vision: "What Red Bull stands for is that it 'gives you wings ...' which means that it provides skills, abilities, power, etc., to achieve whatever you want to. It is an invitation as well as a request to be active, performance-oriented, alert and to take on challenges. When you work or study, do your very best. When you do sports, go for your limits. When you have fun or just relax, be aware of it and appreciate it."

From that unique vision, Mateschitz went on to create sporting and entertainment events that imbedded and connected the story of the brand to compelling *experiences* carefully designed to "give you wings." These include the literal translation of that quest into air shows, as well as a vast sports and entertainment complex with accompanying documentary content distributed globally to Red Bull enthusiasts. The company also owns two Formula 1 racing teams, and pro soccer teams in England, Austria, Brazil and the USA to just scratch the surface of all that the brand does to perpetuate and expand on the tie between the brand and action.

All of this makes Red Bull a *story–do* company rather than a *story–tell* company. As Ty Montague puts it, "Story-doing companies don't just practice what they preach – they actually preach by practicing," and ... "This attribute often creates intense loyalty among customers and employees alike." I think it may also be that story doing creates more opportunities to create positive touchpoints that add up to remarkably high experiential moments—those that become defining moments in the customer's mind.

Southwest Airlines is a good example of a story-do company. So is Amazon and Zappos and others in this book. While most companies typically rely on advertising to do their storytelling, many who practice story doing spend very little or no money on paid media because their medium of choice is the people who use the brand. And it works like gangbusters as the most authentic way to spread a brand story.

WE'RE NOT TALKING "JACK AND JILL WENT UP THE HILL"

Story doing is not about written or verbal narrative like nursery rhymes or the kind of stories brands tell you with advertising. When Heinz Ketchup proudly tells you in a commercial that its sauce is "too thick, to rich to run," it's telling you a good story, one that has worked with many, many millions of advertising dollars spent on a one-way communication to make Heinz Ketchup No. 1. But when British soccer fans pay allegiance on Saturday afternoons to their favorite team sponsored by Red Bull, they are getting a story told by action, not just words. And living stories rather than just telling them works for brands as well as it works for you and me and everybody we know.

Montague defines this kind of story as a "metastory." The best way to understand the concept of metastory is to realize that everybody has one, including you, that is told by your actions, the way you speak and dress, the house you live in, the people you choose to hang out with. It's the story of you that a friend would tell a stranger. Montagu suggests: "It's the observed truth of you that emerges from the sum total of all your actions … It is your *true* story that people use to decide what they think of you, whether they want to befriend you, emulate you, ignore you or scorn you." Your metastory is not what *you* say you are. It's the inescapable story *as others see you and put value on the experience of you.*

"HOW DOES IT MAKE YOU FEEL?"

Brands can gauge their possibilities for good, bad or indifferent performance on the simple measure of their ability to generate emotional involvement. That's why your brand's metastory takes on so much importance. Taking into account that good performance is simply the price of entry, what do your customers say about your product? Would they want a second date with it? How about a live-in relationship? Would they take it home to mamma? Would they give it as a gift to their best friend? These are far from silly questions.

You may think your new grommet is the cat's meow, but your opinion doesn't matter. The question even goes far beyond performance or cost. People today want to know something about your brand's character and trustworthiness to do the right thing. Any airline can fly you from A to B, but will the experience leave you with feelings as involving as those

I ascribe to Southwest? Would the expensive nuisance of getting your windshield replaced be as satisfying as I describe the process with Safelight? In effect, does your brand create a fanatical following based on the experience it delivers? Do your customers think of themselves as a tribe the way Red Bull drinkers and Harley Davidson riders do? These things are possible when you create a metastory and build upon it with an ever-improving experience you do rather than simply tell.

INSIGHT—DOING STORIES IS MORE POWERFUL THAN TELLING STORIES.

The difference between storytelling and story doing is illustrated so well with one of my favorite little examples. If you want people to believe you are funny, you don't walk into the room and tell them you are funny. You tell them a joke. Otherwise, how would they *know* you are funny? A brand works in the same way. You don't just tell customers what your brand is in an ad. You demonstrate the truth and value of your brand through real life experiences.

How do you get people to feel that your energy drink will actually give them energy? Of course, the functional product benefits have to deliver what is promised, but competitive brands will eventually perform just as well. The difference is great brands live their brand story by creating emotionally energized moments that customers experience firsthand. The kind of moments that forge customer stories born from the brand experience that will inevitably get passed along to friends and family.

It's the same for any company that wants people to believe it believes in something. The company doesn't just tell its story, it creates encounters or touchpoints in which customers experience its story firsthand in a way that the customers become the story. It's such a powerful thing that you could even take an odd (some would say awful) tasting beverage, call it Red Bull and build it into an amazingly iconic global brand worth more than $4 billion.

CHAPTER 12

Delivering Wow!

IF THERE WAS EVER A HALL OF FAME FOR CUSTOMER VISIONARIES, 41-year-old Tony Hsieh would be way up there in the pantheon. He took the unlikely proposition that people would want to buy shoes sight unseen online or over the phone and turned it into a brand with the equally unlikely name of Zappos worth more than a billion dollars in annual sales. He accomplished this in about ten years by aligning the entire organization around one mission: to provide the best customer service possible that delivers what he calls WOW.

THE TIMES THEY ARE A-CHANGING

I see Tony as a unique representative of his changing times. He grew up seeing monumental social shifts wrought by the digital revolution that so vastly influences how business can now communicate with us one-on-one rather than as a mass. He is also witness to the slow death of the factory management mentality that wants us to shut up and just do what we're told. Something I read on the Zappos's website said it well:

"Organizational democracy is inevitable. The Internet, the demands of generation X and Y to have a voice in the workplace, and the Gallup Organization report that nearly two-thirds of workers are disengaged at work, causing businesses to rethink their management models and embrace a more inclusive style that will lead their industries, boost the bottom line and build a more democratic world."

THE UPSTART STARTUPS

It's fascinating to watch an entirely new generation of digitally-savvy entrepreneurs completely transforming the world of business. It seems as though they leave no stone unturned to upend the old business applecart. It's partly rebelliousness, but it's mainly that they see their way as *the* way to deliver a better, more efficient, more dramatic customer experience while making the world of work more fulfilling for themselves and their associates.

As Ty Montague says in *True Story,* "They live closer to the ground, closer to their customers, and they tend to sense and feel opportunities as much as anything else. Their decisions often begin as pure instinct, and then data is used to validate those instincts. And innovation is in their blood—they know that to succeed they must stand out. They have to *be* different because they can't afford the hundreds of millions of dollars to *say* they are different." I add to this that guts, imagination and an intimate understanding of customer's desires perform as the mothers of necessity.

Guys like Tony and many others now see business as a way to literally change the world as a natural corollary of their and their company's goals and ambitions. This is why they start companies dedicated to some kind of carefully designed quest. They see them as vehicles of transformation that literally touch all of us. They are less likely to do anything just for money than any other previous generation. If this sounds lofty and idealistic it's only because it is. Work has to mean more than a paycheck. They do indeed see starting a company as a way to make a lot of money, but they also see money as a means to improve and expand on the *value of the experience* they deliver to their employees and the customers they serve. What they do for their living has to connect with the values that characterize a truly useful life.

THEY TALK DIFFERENTLY, TOO.

When a bunch of guys saw an opportunity to contribute a new kind of experience in office sharing, they came up with a company they called Grind, and before doing anything else they built the brand story in language filled with what they saw as the brand's emotional benefit. They encapsulated the Grind quest this way: *The end of working for The Man. To catalyze the revolution taking place in the nature of work and help as many people as possible to escape corporate life to work in a new way – outside the system.*

Going further, they realized they could tell their story in the stale, old, pragmatic way that other shared office spaces do or stay true to their quest to change the way things are done. If they really had passion for their quest, then it should naturally have story language that brings it to life in a way that customers would relate to. Here is a sample of the language they use to elevate their story to a quest:

Grind isn't an office, it's the antidote to offices. Grind is a 22nd century platform that helps talent collaborate in a new way: outside the system. A members-only shared workspace and coworking community dedicated to taking all of the frustrations of working the old way and pulverizing them to a dust so fine it actually oils the wheels of the machine. A space that caters to free radicals like you. An idea that puts the funk in functional and some serious flow in your workflow. An experience built around a handful of simple rules: Be ruthless about clutter. Abolish friction. If it ain't broken, make it better anyway. Sweat the details. Then sweat them again. And cling like crazy to the big truths: simplicity, community, work that works. Want to shatter convention? Rock an industry? Want to change the world? Let's get to work. Congratulations. You're in. Welcome to Grind.

Grind is a great example of how the new breed of business builders create a story *before* they get significantly into the hard data, and, as Ty Montague suggests, it's called a metastory because it guides everything the brand stands for. And look at the language. Can you imagine such graphic words coming out of any old-style business model? There's no stilted, maze-like jargon that is too often the trademark of business obfuscation. Plain English tells it like it is. No pulling punches. No hedging bets, and no mention of money—not because the founders don't care about it, but because they know money comes as a *reward* for the delivery of an *engaging experience* rather than a reason for being.

In my last book I wrote about 26-year-old David Carp who recently put $250 million in the pocket of his hoodie when he sold the blogging service Tumblr to Facebook. He was excited to get the money so he could further develop his company. Meanwhile, he continues to live in his cramped apartment in Brooklyn. For the new generation of high-tech wizards, the old idea of conspicuous consumption that was the habit of past business titans is going away. Conspicuous invention and the money to fund it is now the thing. The guys at Grind and others like David Carp and Tony Hsieh are no exception.

Tony and his partners sold Zappos to Amazon for more than $1 billion worth of Amazon stock. How much of it went to him? I have no idea, but you can bet the same amount that Tony will not be retiring to play golf at the country club any time soon. It's a bet you would win. He's too busy figuring out how to use the money to improve the future.

BRING IT ON

Many of the changes in ways to do business wrought by Tony, from the way he looks at customer service to how he finds and engages employees, are becoming legend, and he sees sharing them freely with other businesses as a way to change the world of work and commerce for the universal better.

The major drive is a monomaniacal focus on company culture as the No. 1 priority for success. In his book *Delivering Happiness: A Path To Profits, Passion and Purpose*, Tony writes, "We thought that if we got the culture right, then building our brand to be about customer service would happen naturally on its own."

This is not a one-plus-one-equals two equation; rather, it is a one-plus-one-equals-a-billion-pairs-of-shoes-year equation. As Tony sees it, one feeds the other.

GETTING ON THE PAYROLL

A good way to start an understanding of Zappos's culture is by imagining you were applying for a job in the Las Vegas headquarters. No matter what kind of job you think you might want to do—accounting, phone rep, lawyer, software developer—you would start going through two kinds of interviews. One is the usual looking at relevant experience and fit within the team. Another is a deeper evaluation of your culture fit. It's not just how smart you are; it's *how* you are smart. It's not just how intelligent you are; it's how *emotionally* intelligent you are. If you get past these points, you would then go through culture training, which involves a full four weeks of going over company history, learning the importance of customer service, studying the company's long-term vision and learning the Zappos philosophy. With all the other newbies, you would then get on the phone for two weeks of taking calls from customers. You would have to do this to live and breathe the customer experience as more important than your individual specialty.

NOW COMES THE AMAZING PART

After the first week, you and each of your fellow applicants would be *offered $2,000 to quit!* This is in addition to paying for the time you already worked, and it's a standing offer until the end of the fourth week.

Writes Tony, "We want to make sure that employees are here for more than a paycheck. We want employees that believe in our long-term vision and want to be part of our culture. As it turns out, less than 1 percent of people end up taking the offer."

VALUES TO LIVE BY, NOT JUST WORK BY

It took a long time to distill what Tony and his partners define as their culture, but they finally got it down to ten core values:

1. Deliver WOW through service
2. Embrace and drive change
3. Create fun and a little weirdness
4. Be adventurous, creative, open-minded
5. Pursue growth and learning
6. Build open and honest relationships with communication
7. Build a positive team and family spirit

8. Do more with less
9. Be passionate and determined
10. Be humble

Like many core value statements, this one only jumps to life when you see how each one of them is practiced in ways that astonish even the most seasoned business leaders. Building open and honest relationships with communication, for example, starts with the Zappos Culture Book in which every employee is asked to write an impression of the company in his or her own words. It is published *with no censoring or editing* of even the occasional negative. This book is also used as a reference handout to anybody interested in the company, including job applicants, suppliers, small business owners, etc. Even customers and vendors are allowed to place comments in the book, and many of them do – once again, completely unedited no matter what the content. It's a great way to understand the culture as it is practiced day to day. And it's an equally great way for Tony and his fellow managers to see how their people view what is going on and to take remedial action when necessary.

There is also a monthly employee newsletter called *Ask Anything* in which any employee can ask any question anonymously. It is e-mailed to everybody in the company. Questions asked go from "Who is on the board of directors" to "Where do you see us in three years? How big and where?" to "Do vegetarians eat animal crackers?" No question big or small is left unanswered.

YOUR FUTURE IS ALL YOURS

If you join the company at an entry-level, you will be expected to take certain courses along with mentorship if you want to get promoted. The usual practice of annual performance reviews does not work here. Do what is required for your personal growth and skills and you can reasonably expect to get into a senior position within five years, and often less. This fits the philosophy that hiring from within is preferable to looking outside for more senior staff. It's what Tony calls building assets through a *pipeline* of talent in every department. Twenty-eight courses are offered with novel kinds of instruction in such things as The Science of Happiness, Tribal Leadership and Leadership Essentials, as well training in HR, Intro to Finance, Communications and Public Speaking. I know of no other company that does this kind of care and feeding of employee ambition for the good of the individual with benefits for the whole team. For individual employees, it means they can track their own career path and pay level as they improve their skills. For the company, it means a never-ending supply of dedicated talent.

SUPPLIER HEAVEN

Zappos people consider their relationships with vendors to be one of the key components of Zappos's success. Rather than treat them like mere suppliers, they are given the respect and courtesy and collaborative concern one would give to a valued partner. And it's the little things that have a habit of ending up exemplifying the Golden Rule in the way people are treated.

When vendors fly to Las Vegas for meetings in Zappos's offices, they are greeted by one of Zappos's shuttles. If it is the first time, they get a tour, along with drinks and snacks – anything to make them feel comfortable. Communication with them is as open as it is with any employee; in fact, suppliers have access to an "extranet" that allows them to see Zappos's inventory levels, sales figures and even profitability! They can write suggested orders for buyers to approve. They can communicate with the creative team. Up to a thousand vendors are invited to the annual Vendor Appreciation party and golf tournaments. At every turn, they are considered valued members of the Zappos family.

MORE EYES ON THE BALL

It's fair to say that suppliers help Zappos's people run their business and play a role in keeping the machine running smoothly. This includes the people at Wells Fargo and UPS, both long-time partners who value mutual loyalty. It's another testament to the power of culture as it permeates every aspect of the brands intent to share generously on a decent, human level that wins friends and ambassadors. This clear thinking is truly impressive and seems like such an obvious way to go—one that is not often on the radar of companies as an essential issue of culture.

WHAT IT ALL ADDS UP TO

Of course, the payoff on all this enlightened operating procedure is the generation of a remarkable customer experience. By fostering the well-being of all the people who take care of the customers, you get people eager and willing to go the extra mile for the customers who make it all possible.

For example, most call centers measure employee performance based on how many calls each rep can take in a day, which is a poor way to foster customer care. Not at Zappos. Going above and beyond for every customer means no written scripts. Reps are encouraged to develop a personal and emotional connection in their own way, which makes the old-fashioned phone call a powerful branding device, even in a high tech world. One customer call actually lasted six hours! And as a kind of test, Tony and friends once called anonymously to find out if a rep could advise him on where to get a late-night pizza in Santa Monica. The rep put him on hold and took all of two minutes to come through with five choices. People apparently call for reasons that have nothing to do with shoes and they always get a cheery response.

If a customer calls about a style and size of shoe not in stock, the rep is trained to research at least three competitors and pass the information on. The loss of a sale is not as important as creating a memorable experience and building a lifelong relationship one phone call at a time.

Order a pair of shoes and you can pretty much count on getting them the next day, sometimes within eight hours. If they don't suit your fancy when you see them in the flesh, you can return them for free, and you can do this up to a year after you buy. Wow indeed!

CREATING FUN AND A LITTLE WEIRDNESS

Take a tour of Zappos's headquarters and you will find everybody delighted to see you. You might run into a makeshift bowling alley made by the software developers. You could see a parade to celebrate Octoberfest or people dressed as pirates. A petting zoo, a karaoke session, a hot dog picnic or a popcorn machine dressed up as a robot in the lobby. We saw this kind of fun and games in the Cognex story and the positive effect it has on morale and creating a strong community. As a cultural artifact, it is a priceless way to create relationships, teamwork and cohesion with random acts of WOW.

AMAZON AS PARTNER

Talks with Amazon CEO Jeff Bezos began in early 2009 and coincided with Zappos's board members wanting to cash in on their investment. Jeff first suggested buying Zappos for cash, but Tony and his partners knew that selling was not their goal. They wanted to continue building the brand and its culture. They wanted to continue to feel like owners, which is why they pushed hard for an all-stock transaction that was much more in the spirit of a marriage and analogous to a couple getting a joint bank account. It was good for everybody—a win-win situation good for Amazon, the board, employees and shareholders. Once more we see the good of the common welfare as the true source of the why and the way these guys work.

Both Amazon and Zappos have a deep tradition of placing great value on customer welfare, albeit with slightly different approaches. As Tony says, "We thought of Zappos as being more high-touch, and Amazon being more high-tech." But it was clear that with a mutually committed focus on the customer, the marriage was not the kind of culture clash that can ruin many corporate mergers. Being a revolutionary kind of brand-builder in his own right, Jeff Bezos pledged that he would not want to change the successful Zappos culture that is so important to Tony and friends, one that feels more like a real, caring family than just a business.

SHARING THE WEALTH

A surprising benefit of the arrangement was that rather than a cause for doubt and anxiety, the merger announcement came as good news to employees. During the negotiation, legal considerations forbid any public discussion. This troubled Tony and his partners because they had always pursued the path of an open and inclusive culture. When the announcement was delivered, they went to great pains to assure all staff that the arrangement with Amazon included the continuation of business as usual, that all employees were still in control of their own destiny and that nobody was going to lose their job. And in fact, *every* employee would receive a new Amazon Kindle e-reader and a cash bonus of $10,000!

SHARING THE WEALTH IN OTHER WAYS

The more the stories of "Tony's social experiments" are exposed, the more other companies want to know about them, and Zappos's people are willing to oblige. Stunning financial results achieved so rapidly had a lot do with attracting attention, as does consistently making the Fortune 500 list of Best Companies to Work For. What other companies learn from Zappos, however, might come as a surprise when they discover that it is all about developing and nurturing a culture that, in Zappos's case, was in the pursuit of an astonishing quest. The evolution of that mission has gone from *largest selection of shoes* in 1999, to *customer service* in 2003, to *core values* as a platform in 2005, to *personal emotional connection* in 2007 to *delivering happiness to the world* in 2009.

"Happiness in a box" is how customers think of a Zappos shipment. It's easy to see how employees see the company as the pursuit of happiness in and out of office hours, and even for suppliers it's hard to imagine a happier, more caring business relationship. What might sound like a very big stretch for a shoe company's mission is indeed the very real pursuit of that usually elusive condition we call shared happiness. It's quite remarkable and sets an example of how to prosper in the sometimes-cynical world of for-profit business. A mantra of profit, passion and purpose works as an effective combination with great favor for Zappos's people and customers. The question you might now ask is can you work similar magic in your own way for your business?

While writing the Zappos story, I kept wondering how it would be to work there as phone rep. It's a job I have a hard time imagining as a calling (no pun intended), but I can see how it could become one at Zappos. Becoming a linchpin kind of person has less to do with an actual job and more to do with how the job is approached. Being a phone rep at Zappos requires emotional intelligence and provides emotional rewards. People who do it well indeed create happiness by making personal, human connections with the gift of their full attention, with brightening someone's day, with the surprise of a really caring attitude, and it can only be done well when the rep feels free to do it in his or her own way. When everybody in a company invests with emotional intelligence in his or her own way, you create something priceless. You create a small army of linchpins. You create a mind-blowing culture like Zappos.

INSIGHT—THE LITTLE THINGS YOU DO CAN CREATE A BIG WOW!

I owned a website development company and was very active in the Internet boom of the late 1990s. I remember hearing the notion of selling shoes online and thinking it would never work because people simply must try on shoes before they buy them. It was crazy and impossible, just more Internet hype. It never really crossed my mind that the problem could easily be solved by removing the shipping and return shipping obstacles. Looking back now, it was a little thing even then had I taken time to think outside the box for just a moment.

Thinking outside the box isn't as difficult as it may seem. You just have to realize how important it is and be willing to do it. Thinking outside the box is simply a matter of looking beyond the way you've always done things and past the operations and logistics sacred cows acquired over time by your industry and your business. Everyone wants his or her customers to buy more. I guarantee if you make it easier, more enjoyable and more rewarding to buy from you, your customers will do it more often. How crazy is that?

CHAPTER 13

What Matters Most?

I REMEMBER A LONG-DISTANCE PHONE COMPANY COMMERCIAL that had as its theme line, "Reach out and touch someone." When you think about it, this is the literal expression of what all brands attempt to do to create customer loyalty and advocacy.

What brands do to touch customers and build trust with the experience of their brands brings to mind the advice of poet Maya Angelou: "People will forget what you said, people will forget what you did, but people will never forget how you made them feel."

In many ways, Maya's reminder is the ultimate message of this book—the very point of developing a true, compelling brand story is to inspire employees and attract an enthusiastic customer following.

Here's the point missed by so many companies and their brands. Success hinges *entirely* on the touchpoints, often the little things, that you either do or don't do along the customer's journey with your brand. The truth of your story, your brand and your company is exposed in the little things you do—not the big things you say. Is your story true? How does your brand experience make your customers feel? Can they trust your brand to do what it promises? Never forget that what you do speaks so loudly that customers can barely hear what you have to say.

A BLINDING GLIMPSE OF THE OBVIOUS

There may come a time when everything we do is managed by robots that can do no wrong, but before that sad prospect ever becomes reality, no brand will get everything right 100 percent of the time. Big and little things can and will go awry along the path of the customer's experience.

Fortunately, people don't expect companies and brands to be perfect. They just expect them to do what they say they will. When things do go wrong, most people are reasonable and quick to forgive provided the company does the right thing; accepts responsibility and tries to fix the problem. In truth, many of the most loyal customers are created in these moments when a brand proves it can and will do the right thing. Most of the stories in this book exemplify this human truth.

These stories also reveal something very significant and extremely useful. Some brand experiences along the customer's journey are more emotional—and thus much more important—than others. This is valuable to know because it means companies can focus on the moments that matter most instead of futilely struggling to monitor and manage dozens, hundreds or maybe thousands of touchpoints when many scarcely matter at all. Our research at Brandtrust with thousands of people confirms only a handful of the experiences along a customer's journey with a brand are truly significant and actually contribute to forming the emotional bonds that establish loyalty and advocacy.

The Sloan Management Review confirms, "Organizations in general have found success in identifying and focusing on points in the service cycle where emotions tend to be high. Rather than include everything, it helps to simplify by concentrating on the strong positives and negatives." In other words, your customers' positive experience can indeed be narrowed down to what are usually a few little things that mean a lot. Inevitably, these little things boil down to human things—those that make us feel something positive about ourselves. Things that, in many cases, don't actually cost anything at all—beyond an enduring commitment to do the right thing for your customers.

Still, I saw a recent Bain and Company survey in which 80 percent of the companies surveyed believed they delivered superior customer experience, while only 8 percent of their customers agreed. For competitive reasons, companies are focused on customers like never before but apparently not on the things that matter to customers. It is troubling when you think about the time, money and opportunities squandered on well-intentioned but misguided customer experience programs knowing there are smarter, more effective and much less expensive solutions. As Sir Arthur Conan Doyle's Sherlock Holmes warned, "There is nothing as deceptive as an obvious fact."

PEAK EXPERIENCES

You don't have to be a business genius to recognize that emotions have the ruling influence on what customers remember. But it is extremely useful to know that what they remember is determined by the intensity of emotions created *within* a particular moment—not the entire overall experience.

Give two groups of kids a great chocolate candy bar and they will be happy. Then give only one of the groups an inexpensive piece of hard candy. Logically, we think the kids who get two pieces of candy will naturally be happier—they have more candy! Right? But, no they aren't. Actually, when scientists conduct this very experiment, the kids that receive two pieces of candy are less satisfied.

Nobel laureate and father of behavioral economics, Daniel Kahneman, described this phenomenon as the Peak-End Rule, explaining how experiences are judged almost entirely on the intensity of emotions at their peak moments coupled with the end point or resolution of the experience. Our brains are not equipped to store and retain a complete end-to-end customer experience, only the parts that are emotionally salient. So a positive experience—the chocolate candy bar—is diminished and turns negative when a cheap piece of hard candy follows it and is the last moment in the experience. Virtually every other aspect of the experience appears to be forgotten, including the overall pleasantness or unpleasantness of the entire experience.

Just for example, a trip to the grocery involves countless touchpoints for a customer, including emotional rewards such as finding a new product that provides healthy meal solutions for hard-to-please kids, the satisfaction of checking everything off the list and completing her shopping task, frustrations about out-of-stock items, a confusing store layout, a surly checkout girl and difficulty returning a shopping cart to the queue. She will take the whole experience in stride and think nothing of it since she is accustomed to the overall experience of grocery shopping. But the emotional parts of her mind will not forget even subtle disappointments that evoke the feeling, without ever thinking of it consciously, that she should go to a different grocery store the next time. Or when the shopping experience has no emotional rewards, she will seek them elsewhere without even knowing why.

The touchpoints with the most positive or negative emotional intensity, and the end or resolution of these specific peak moments, have a disproportionate influence on the customer's overall experience. This is very good news for brands that are willing to take the time to identify and enhance the peak moments along their customer's journey. Those who identify their customer's peak moments can stop wasting time and energy on things that don't matter nearly as much. They can intensely focus on improving and optimizing the critical Peak-End moments that mean the most to how the customer feels about your brand.

In our work for many major brands, we consistently see much of what actually creates a successful brand is the ability to deeply understand the psychology of the handful of peak emotional moments in their customer's experience. These are the moments that create and sustain loyalty while increasing the lifetime value of a customer. These are the moments that unlock the secrets to extraordinary customer experience and high growth brands.

EMOTIONAL INTENSITY AND THE POWER OF EXPERIENCES

Customer interactions, intentionally or unintentionally, shape the customer's perceptions for good or bad. We can be very sure of the obvious: customers prefer brand encounters when the peak-end experiences have positive emotional clout. Even television commercials that induce positive feelings rate better when the commercials have high peaks of intensity and strong positive endings.

To create memorable moments, you have to know which touchpoints are the most intense and which underlying emotions trigger the intensity. A good example is seen in London where the rail authorities realized a negative experience was created while commuters waited for Metro trains to arrive at their station. On deeper discovery, it turned out the reason why this experience was causing anxiety wasn't as much from the waiting as not knowing when the next train would arrive. Would it be five minutes or twenty? Once officials installed digital displays indicating the time until the next train arrived, customer experience ratings improved. The trains weren't any more on time, but the negative emotional angst in the moment was greatly diminished. In retrospect, it's easy to see how replacing ambiguity with order reduces anxiety, but it took decades of poor customer experience before anyone realized why this key emotional insight could be used to design a dramatically improved customer experience.

To successfully shape the customer's journey, it's important to understand more than *what* customers are responding to. It's essential to understand *why*. Knowing why enables companies to optimize touchpoints to fulfill the most essential motivations, thus creating experiences that consistently generate customer satisfaction and, in turn, brand loyalty.

HOW WE THINK WE THINK AND HOW WE REALLY THINK

Throughout your lifetime, your nonconscious mind stores incomprehensible amounts of information by categorizing and cataloguing memories according to the nature and intensity of the emotion associated with them. The neural activity that creates and recalls these memories can be stimulated in a variety of ways—by touch, sound, sight, smell, taste, feeling or any sensory experience.

Whenever the brain processes new stimuli generated by any experience, the subconscious brain automatically associates the sensation of the encounter with related memories, and it does this neurologically. In order for you to function without stumbling over every little decision you have to make in the course of a normal day, most of your mental processing occurs beyond your awareness in your nonconscious mind. Think of it this way: if you had to consciously process everything that occurs every moment of every day, your head would explode. This has led behavioral scientists to realize that customer attitudes, feelings, perceptions and behaviors in response to experiences are governed primarily by nonconscious influences—not by conscious thoughts. To all the people you know out there who place great store in their ability to do everything in their lives based on logic, reasoning and self-determination, this might come as a nasty shock.

Most of the stuff we do we simply do not have to think about, like looking both ways before crossing the street, or driving to work on what seems like automatic pilot while we're plotting how to ask the boss for a raise and remembering that we have to pick up the dry cleaning and little Johnny's dental appointment is tomorrow, and oh, red light ahead so apply the brakes. Most of it takes place in the nonconscious mechanisms of our brains that make many reactions automatic, like not having to think about running for our lives when buzzed by a bumblebee.

This is why when we associate emotion with brands we have to understand that much of it is deeply rooted in customers' nonconscious memories. Your precious brand is rarely top of mind. We do not feel a need for a deeply conscious relationship with our dishwasher detergent. We do indeed have some kind of feeling about it, but it's mostly outside of our immediate awareness and beyond what conventional research techniques can reveal. Consequently, rational metrics for customer experiences simply cannot provide the deep insights necessary to understand what represents an emotionally resonant moment. Oddly enough, the relationship you have formed with your dishwasher detergent, while hardly life changing, may be more meaningful than you're aware of on a conscious level. From research we've done in this product category, I can assure you it is.

I've mentioned Morton's Salt is a perfect example to explain how we feel more deeply about ordinary brands than we understand consciously. The product is in no way different from any other brand of salt. They all conform to the same formula for sodium chloride, yet Morton's has a commanding share of the market simply because it is likely the brand your mother and grandmother used, and they are how you first experienced a brand of salt. The emotion you have for them is still connected to Morton's because no other salt brand has done anything to dissuade your feelings. In a research setting, you can inform people store brand salt is thirty percent cheaper and is actually identical to

Morton's, and most of them will still insist on Morton's. Even though it's just salt, apparently we have deeper feelings for Morton's salt than we can credibly fathom!

Along similar lines, I ran into a friend in my drugstore buying Tylenol. I pointed out to him that I use the generic drugstore brand because it's exactly the same, that it might even be made by Tylenol and that it was considerably less expensive. He would have none of it. He happily paid more for his precious painkiller and has probably never given his allegiance more than a passing nod of a conscious thought to his attachment to the brand.

VOICE OF CUSTOMER VERSUS MIND OF CUSTOMER

Many marketers rely on the voice of the customer (VOC) for feedback—usually by asking questions about the product category, functional needs and brand encounters. There are two problems with this, and both need to be taken quite seriously. First, if most of what drives our behavior is nonconscious, we can't possibly provide a reliable response. Secondly, the mere act of asking a direct question primes the respondent's conscious mind to give what they hope is the "correct" answer. The conscious mind often supports this answer with a rationale that sounds right but masks the true, underlying nonconscious emotions that actually drive feelings, preferences and behavior. In fact, our work at Brandtrust has confirmed many times over that if you need to know why someone believes or behaves in a certain way, the worst thing you can do is ask them about it. This problem is often compounded in focus group research sessions where one alpha character hogs the show, intimidates the other participants and triggers inaccurate discussions, thus delivering research that can be badly flawed.

Compounding all of this is the fact that word choice, context and the sequence of questions can prime respondents about what the "correct" answer is without either the researcher or respondent being aware of it. We know that up to 80 percent of the messages and meanings we convey to one another are expressed in nonverbal ways, such as through gestures, body posture, intonation, distance, eye contact and pupil dilation. For these reasons, it's critically important to shift your mental model from "voice of the customer" to "mind of the customer" and probe it with research methodologies that do not misdirect or prime the nonconscious mind.

GO DEEPER

As mentioned briefly earlier, Emotional Inquiry® is a form of research utilized by our teams at Brandtrust designed to discover the deeper, richer why's underlying the customer's nonconscious motivations. Interviewers with strong social science backgrounds use visualization and relaxation techniques, probing rather than prompting. Respondents describe what they see and experience in their memories instead of answering direct questions.

Over the course of one-on-one interviews, patterns emerge that help researchers to isolate and describe emotional intensity during peak moments across various touchpoints. More importantly, our researchers are able to identify and understand the nonconscious why's that cause these feelings. These insights make it possible to design customer encounters that are so emotionally rewarding they can create irrational loyalty for your brand. Touchpoints might include the moment a customer walks into your store, your hotel lobby or your clinic. It could be the first moments on the phone with you or visiting your website. It might be the way your people initiate contact if your business involves making house calls. These can be the few critical moments when the rubber might indeed be hitting the road with little things that loom very large in the customer's experience and feeling about you and your brand. These critical moments are rarely identified with standard research techniques that only scratch the conscious surface.

CAUGHT, NOT TAUGHT

Another key step in delivering a peak customer experience is building empathy with the customers you serve. Project teams are usually very busy. They are stretched thin—running on tight budgets and even tighter deadlines. There is rarely time in the schedule to really think about customers, let alone invest any significant time with them. Yet this is exactly the type of skill acquisition that helps teams to work more efficiently and focus on what really matters to the people they serve. It can truly shift the way you look at your business and spark fresh thinking rooted in empathy and understanding. It's about defining what actions will be directed, to whom and how they will be enacted. From this strategic vision you can concentrate on the most critical touchpoints that will achieve the right responses.

It's also important to get top management on board to see the light as keenly as the person who answers the phone to take orders, complaints, etc. Leaders must encourage employees to emotionally own any kind of change initiative for it to be successful. Only they can make it happen. Managing the customer experience is something that has to be personally internalized. It requires keen emotional instinct simply because problems arise that can't always be anticipated. They must be *caught, not taught.*

To make sure the new brand position is caught, not taught, the basic idea is to use the human truths revealed through employee and customer research to focus individuals and organizations around what works. Creating this focus is more than a project; it has to be a way of life, and to become one, it is never finished. It continuously drives improvement. It's the kind of command of key touchpoint experiences well illustrated by what goes on at Zappos, where empathy with customers is indeed a natural way of life.

It's one thing to articulate a promise of great care and another altogether to live that promise. Only when it becomes the driving force of the brand story and an essential part of the brand quest, will it stick like glue, and there is no magic formula, just consistent case-by-case deep digging. Here are a few more examples of how emotional insights enabled companies to build brand preference and loyalty by improving critical moments along the customer's journey.

WHEN THE POWER GOES OFF

What could a major public utility company do to raise customer satisfaction scores consistently ranking in the 90th percentile? Senior managers, whose performance evaluations were based on increased customer satisfaction, wanted to know. It's difficult to improve satisfaction when the only time people think of a utility is when there is a problem or power outage. Emotional Inquiry revealed a critical, singular positive peak experience recalled by numerous customers. Oddly enough, it involved cookies.

Many years ago, back in the days when energy consumption was encouraged instead of energy conservation, the company had distributed free cookie recipe booklets each year around the holidays. This nice little practice had been abandoned somewhere along the line, but was revived when our research revealed this seemingly frivolous touchpoint had profound emotional wallop. This and other initiatives suggested by the research created incremental gains in customer satisfaction. This shows how rational analysis is never enough; in fact, rational statistical analyses had consistently missed this serendipitous little revelation altogether.

Another brand that turns an unwanted encounter into a peak experience is Safelight, featured earlier in this book. Nobody looks forward to getting a windshield replaced, but sensitivity on the part of Safelight technicians makes it acceptable and even positively memorable.

RESTORING LOST MARKET SHARE

A top beverage brand had significant market share erosion occurring in critical U.S. markets. Scanner data clearly indicated what was happening, but the beverage maker could not explain why. Brandtrust conducted an emotional touchpoint analysis to figure out what was going on. We discovered peak emotional problems involving packaging, merchandising and stock counts that created a poor customer experience that also betrayed the brand's promise on a deeper nonconscious level. Understanding the emotional side of the peak moments was critical in fixing what was wrong. Share erosion stopped in short order after the changes were implemented.

REVVING UP AN ICONIC BRAND PROMISE

One of the world's top motorcycle brands worked with Brandtrust to understand their customers' emotional motivations for owning this well-loved brand. Revealing the deeper psychological reasons that create the passion for the brand also pointed to the importance of the entire life cycle and ecosystem of the brand experience. We identified specific dealer encounters occurring while customers are shopping, purchasing and maintaining motorcycles that are critical peak-moment touchpoints. Our discoveries helped this client find new approaches for dealer training and communications that greatly improve the customer's peak experiences at the critical source of purchase.

DUSTING THE PLANTS

A large healthcare company struggled to understand why they could not improve patient satisfaction scores in several specialty areas. Many things were tried, but still the scores refused to budge. Brandtrust was engaged to conduct studies, along with a comprehensive touchpoint analysis of the patient's end-to-end experience. We discovered patients were very approving of the human touch evident throughout the facilities, but neglected aesthetic nuances were creating negative impressions, affecting underlying feelings about the facility and the care that might be provided in such an environment. Something as subtle as dust on the plants suggests if you can't take care of the plants, can you take care of people? Corrective actions were taken to improve the unappealing aesthetics and, over time, satisfaction scores began to increase. This shows that simple, little things do indeed often mean more than we ever know until we probe with the delicacy of a brain surgeon into feelings the customer might not be able to articulate with direct questioning.

FOCUS AND ENERGY MAKE ALL THE DIFFERENCE

The idea that drives our work and should drive yours is that great brand and customer experience is driven by focus and energy. The Peak-End Rule scientifically substantiates the need to focus on the most meaningful moments of customer experience. The identification of what matters most to customers provides clarity and focuses energy to the vision, mission, brand promise or to the metastory of the brand quest. Our clients respond very positively to the idea of peak moments because it helps them *feel* the focus, makes it possible to effect positive change in their customers' experience without needless complexity.

The companies I cite in this book are the ones that take the time to figure out what matters most to their customers and employees, and then laser focuses the company's people and energies on those things. This tight focus is what makes these companies more successful in finding positive experiences for their employees and customers. Things that don't matter do not distract them, nor do they squander resources or opportunities on things that fail to provide a high return on the energies and resources they invest.

THE POLISHED APPLE

One story I tell that helps people get it is Apple. People leap to the assumption that Apple's success is all about product innovation, but the truth is their products are never the first ones in the category. Not the first personal computer, laptop, music player, smart phone, tablet, not the first of anything. The genius of Apple is creating the *experience* the customer wants and hopes for. iPod was not the first MP3 player, and there were good products on the market when it was introduced. It did not sell very well in its first year on the market. What Steve Jobs understood was that the experience of downloading music was frustrating to the point that people just would not do it. So, Apple created iTunes to enable easy access to music and other content. The experience was the innovation, not the product. Apple demonstrates the peak-end factors better than practically any brand. They understand the emotional anxieties and rewards around the peak moments of customers feeling like the technology won't work or it will make them feel stupid. That's why the products are designed elegantly to look and feel easy to operate (and they are), and Apple understands the out-of-the-box experience better than anyone. There is a lot of anxiety and potential emotional reward in that moment, so Apple makes the packaging and the whole unpacking experience exquisite to the point that people actually keep their Apple boxes forever. (Full disclosure: I have owned five iPhones and cannot bear to throw any of the beautifully-designed boxes away).

I have worked with large technology companies that think Apple wastes money with too much emphasis on design. I do my best to dissuade them of this notion. Design for simplicity and elegance is the lifeblood of the experience of this iconic brand.

So, Apple, as any good brand, really boils down to a handful of peak moments on which they focus all of their energy. These moments become the few things that people remember and how we create our emotional mental models for the brand. It's never a whole litany of things we use to judge a brand; it's a few little moments that matter most. The moments explain why I hear people all the time say with real affection, "I *love* my iPhone," and "My iPad is my friend."

INSIGHT—IT'S OBVIOUS: FOCUS YOUR ENERGY ON WHAT MATTERS MOST.

As an adviser to many top brands, I am privileged to witness the internal workings of numerous large corporations. Most are truly impressive in their ability to navigate incredible business complexities. Yet, the skills required to juggle so much complexity actually create distractions that blow your brand off course. When your brand loses its way, the most important and most obvious things—those that absolutely matter more than anything else—become obscured. It is obvious that losing focus is detrimental to any business and particularly to a brand. But as we consult and advise our client partners, we see the loss of focus happening every day. This in spite of what we know is that the best brands are the best because they are clearly better at identifying and focusing their most intense energies on what matters most. Time and again we see the most successful brands striving to master these five critical aspects of managing and growing their business.

1. Deeply understanding what matters most to customers and employees.
2. Using that understanding to create a laser focus that everyone can rally around—higher calling, heroic cause, brand quest, badge of honor, etc..
3. Crafting, sharing and *doing* the story of the brand quest relentlessly in every thing the company does.
4. Using a Peak-End approach to figure out which moments matter most in the customer and employee's experience.
5. Relentlessly focusing on the peaks or moments that matter most and working continuously to improve them.

CHAPTER 14

Ben's Big Secret

I DIDN'T KNOW THE GUY SITTING QUIETLY NEAR THE BACK OF THE room, but I suspected he wasn't paying much attention to my presentation. I think he was doodling.

Brandtrust, was less than a year old at the time and this meeting was an important opportunity for us. My friend, Barb Ford, the vice president of advertising for Kraft Foods, had given us a chance to present our capabilities to a few of their key people.

The presentation went smoothly and there were several questions about how we approached projects as a hybrid research and strategy firm. I answered their questions and we chatted a bit about the ways Kraft might best use our services. The same guy in the back of the room did not say anything, and really didn't even acknowledge our discussion. I didn't think much of it one way or the other, but it sure seemed like he wasn't particularly impressed or interested.

A few weeks later, he called, mentioned sitting in on the presentation, and wanted to talk about how we might address an intriguing and complex challenge Kraft was exploring in the organic dairy space. We had a long, interesting discussion and it was obvious, despite my initial impression, he had been listening very closely during my presentation. As it turned out, he remembered some things even better than I did.

That attentiveness is one of the things I've grown to appreciate about Ben Brenton. It's an important indicator of how he approaches innovation and how he manages to create so many successful new products year in and year out. It's just one reason why I'm convinced that he is among the smartest and best of all the innovation people we work with. And, why we have learned a lot from him.

You might not guess it at first glance, but Ben is a committed triathlete who works at staying in shape by riding his bike to and from work, thirty miles each way. You might soon discover, upon speaking with him, that he's from Nebraska and a passionate Cornhusker football fan, once he dons his favorite bright red ball cap emblazoned with a big white N.

Ben's degrees from the University of Nebraska include a BS in Microbiology and a MS in Microbial Genetics. He also earned a PhD in Food Science and Nutrition from the University of Massachusetts that he utilized extensively as director of innovation for Kraft Foods and PepsiCo. With all that food experience, it's all the more remarkable that Ben is currently the chief innovation officer for Snap-on Tools.

We've worked with him for more than fifteen years at Kraft, Pepsi and now Snap-on, collaborating closely to create new products and innovation processes, including rapid immersion and prototyping that makes it possible to research, ideate, test, iterate and retest ideas in highly efficient short bursts. Ben's need to come up with several hundred new concepts each year prompted us to innovate our own innovation processes.

Throughout our many adventures, we've had far more successes than failures. Our journey with Ben has been enlightening, satisfying and successful because we've become kindred spirits in what we believe about innovation and how we approach it. In particular, the belief that the practice of innovation should be viewed much more broadly and seen as a process of innovating customer experiences rather than just developing new products. Some of the most successful innovations are not new products at all, but enhancements that make it easier or better to utilize existing products. For example, sometimes a tool just needs to feel better in the customer's hand. It's not a new tool or even a new way of using it, but it is a completely new experience for the customer.

We've learned and shared a lot about what works and what does not. Many of our clients who want to innovate better and more often ask, "What's Ben's secret?" We've observed that it seems to come down to three essential behaviors.

1. GO DEEP

Ben is adamant, as I am, that you must understand customers deeply enough to know them better than they know themselves. He knows firsthand that you cannot just ask people questions if you need to know how they really think and feel, and why they do what they do. He insists you have to immerse yourself in customers' lives and even try to live through product and brand experiences alongside them to truly understand. I've heard him make the point how convinced he is that his team can stay ahead of customer needs and Snap-on's competitors just by getting into customers' heads to truly understand why they do the things they do.

The biggest mistake most companies make with customer research is settling for data instead of demanding true insights. There is nothing wrong with data unless you settle for asking a plethora of survey questions, yet neglect to dig deeper to reveal why the behaviors exist in the first place. Research that delivers only market data is hardly worth the cost. Data rarely tells you why customers do what they do and, rest assured, your competitors have similar market data. It's one thing to gather facts and analyze patterns in the data, but it's another thing altogether to discover real human insights that deliver competitive advantage to the business.

Ben also knows people say one thing and do another. People don't know their own minds and can't predict what they will do. Yet conventional market research persists in asking respondents what they think and to predict their future behaviors. What people think is the correct answer to a research question does marketing researchers and strategists very little good. In fact, it frequently leads them astray. From my experience, I would wager this is the single greatest explanation for why so many extensively tested new products fail.

This is why it is critical to utilize research methods that allow you to explore nonconscious motivations, people's unarticulated desires and needs. It means you have to reveal how certain experiences created and framed the beliefs and emotions that influence customers' behaviors. But it is dark (and scary) inside people's minds, and traditional market researchers do not know their way around in there. Which may explain why they tend to recommend and settle for shallow, one-dimensional research that provides answers to what is happening, but never why it is happening. Yet, if we don't discover why people do what they do, we'll never meet their unarticulated desires and needs. We will fail to find any competitive advantage in the marketplace and will never create the experiences that inspire loyalty.

This explains why I am first and foremost a marketer, but over the last fifteen years have also become an applied social and behavioral science practitioner with expertise at getting into people's heads. And, once again, it's why I advocate so strongly that marketers, who need to discover deep insights and true advantage must shift their own mental models from the "voice of the customer" to the "mind of the customer"—because that's where the real insights are.

To Ben, this was a bit of a revelation. This notion of the need for deeper insight is what he took away from that very first presentation when I assumed he wasn't listening. It convinced him that better innovation, better product and brand experiences demanded that he change the way he thinks about how customers think. This realization convinced Ben that many of the best ideas are deeply rooted in our nonconscious memories. That's when he says he became "determined to stop buying research and start buying insights," because the best ideas are rarely top-of-mind. We do not naturally process innovations in a superficially conscious way. We do indeed have some kind of feeling about it, but it's mostly outside of our immediate awareness, and well beyond what conventional research techniques can reveal. Consequently, rational approaches simply cannot provide the deep insights necessary to understand what represents an emotionally resonant customer experience or a meaningful innovation.

For example, together we've discovered insights into motivations that are beyond anything we as researchers and consultants ever thought possible—namely, that tools are much more than devices to fix things. They represent a fascinating rite of passage on the part of men who grew up watching their role models work with tools. Boys live for the moment when they are asked to help. Tools represent strength, reliability and power. Men strive to emulate the masculine characteristics embodied by their tools.

2. HMM ... THAT'S INTERESTING

Curiosity opens your mind to new possibilities and fresh connections, and I've observed that Ben is insatiably curious about many things. For example, he is fascinated with the variety in types and brands of beers. This is not a casual curiosity since it includes sampling and rating beers as he travels around the world. At last count he has tasted, rated and cataloged more than 3,000 beers, which he publishes in the Brenton Beer Guide available on iTunes. When he started at Snap-on, his first initiative was to create and develop a new innovation center. Unwilling to settle with his own extensive innovation experience, he interviewed twenty corporations about their innovation centers and spent several months going out and visiting many of the best innovation facilities around. Since the opening of Snap-on's Innovation Works, he has hosted more than a dozen companies looking to build their own centers.

Many of our clients hire us to conduct our special brand of customer research—emotional studies, observations, immersions and ethnographies—because they rarely spend any time at all with customers. This is what we often refer to as the idea that marketers, innovation and customer experience managers must become "method marketers" in the same way method actors strive to become their characters. Generating new products or improved customer experiences rarely happens in the office without first seeing and understanding why customers get up in the morning and try to do a good job every day.

Ben believes you can only build deep customer empathy firsthand. He typically spends sixty to seventy days a year in the field talking and visiting with Snap-on customers, in their bays, observing them as they work with tools. An advocate for the power of observation, he watches closely to see what others don't see to reveal what customers can rarely articulate. He believes you must get out there and notice everything, because you never know when an experience will pique your curiosity and spark a connection to a great idea. In his case, literally get your hands dirty.

Ben's quest to get out there includes being, like me, an avid reader, including Grant McCraken's book *Culturematic*, which offers a refreshing take on how to think differently about innovation by viewing it more intentionally through the lens of culture. McCraken urges, "The corporation continues to think of innovation as R&D, as something that comes out of the lab. This is apt, as long as we remember that the lab is the world."

For those who want to tap the power of our dynamic culture, McCraken proposes that Culturematics are probes of the possible, a way to investigate the future. "We fire them into the world to see what phones home. Think of them as little ingenuity machines that let us test the world, discover meaning and unleash value."

Given the dismal record of new products, it makes sense that companies should embrace fresh approaches to innovation. McCraken submits the reason for such poor results is because the business world has tried to "domesticate" new ideas. But ideas don't like to be managed—they prefer to range free. They're messy, unconventional, slippery little devils that tend to show up in the most unpredictable places.

Ben's prescription is very similar. He becomes a Culturematic by starting small and simply noticing things—noticing everything. He treats the world as a laboratory where we experiment with new ideas that force him to think about things he never set out to consider. As McCraken proclaims, "This is evolutionary strategy, iterative innovation and rapid prototyping all at once … the perfect antidote to a world where we cannot guess what's coming next."

McCraken's easiest and most appealing suggestion for discovering more innovative ideas is to become hyper-aware of anything that causes you to think, "Hmm, that's interesting." And since that's exactly how I would describe Ben's approach, I encourage you to add it to your skill set. What's most interesting is that, if you stay insatiably curious and interested, you're likely to become the most interesting person your friends and colleagues know—a living, breathing Culturematic. Hmm, now that is interesting.

3. RE-EVERYTHING

Ben believes that innovation is born of customer insight. He believes you discover insights by being relentlessly curious about what's really going on out there in the world. He knows getting into customers' heads reveals insight into what truly motivates them, drives their behaviors and decisions. Insight helps him rethink everything, challenge assumptions and chase down suspicions about why customers do what they do. We've noticed he has a kind of sly, crooked smile that signals when he's on to an insight or a hidden truth about customers. He understands the power and the pleasure of insight and has always transformed his teams at Kraft, Pepsi and now Snap-on. He's converted them all—made them zealots for deep customer insight.

Also, Ben is undeniably a scientist at heart—a creative scientist, but a scientist nonetheless. Before he falls in love with any idea, he will rethink everything. He uses customer insights to redefine the problem dozens of times, combine and recombine things that normally don't go together, rethink the possibilities and exhaustively reorder potential solutions until he is convinced it's right. Science is never-ending innovation because it doesn't settle for any one conclusion. Its very nature is to keep rethinking, reconnecting and reexamining. Ben approaches innovation as a creative science that's never settled.

When I try to boil down all the things that convince me that Ben is a great innovator and that we can learn a lot from him, I'm drawn to a line from the movie Dead Poets Society:

> "We must constantly look at things in a different way. Just when you think you know something, you must look at it in a different way. Even though it may seem silly or wrong, you must try. Dare to strike out and find new ground."

I think this is a terrific summary of how Ben approaches the world, and the ideal inspiration for how anyone can be more innovative more often.

Innovation also has a down side when we see the disruption it can cause with old ideas and technologies. A glaring example is the demise of Kodak, the company that invented the portable camera (and, indeed, invented the digital camera) as it went the way of all those slow and unwilling to adapt—eventually declaring bankruptcy in 2012.

I find something quite sad about an iconic brand disappearing from common consciousness. It's a little like losing an old friend and a vital part of our shared life experience. After all, George Eastman Kodak put several generations of family snapshots into the albums of ordinary people in the same way that Henry Ford put the automobile on the road for the pleasure and convenience of our humble ancestors. The treasured experiences of our most personal histories were captured and frozen in time in what we used to call "Kodak moments," an expression that has virtually disappeared from the modern vernacular. To now call them "Instagram moments" or "Facebook moments" simply doesn't have the same ring.

I can't help but wonder what might have happened to Kodak if Ben or someone like him had been working there reexamining, rethinking and reconnecting the dots to help the company reveal their customers' desires and expose something that might have spared the company's downfall.

Oh, and Ben was doodling by the way. He does it all the time, especially when he wants to really focus. Studies have shown it actually improves concentration and helps you remember what you hear. When you're curious, you discover useful things like that. So be insatiably curious and doodle away.

INSIGHT—DARE TO CHANGE THE WAY YOU THINK.

Revealed human truth can profoundly change everything. For example, realizing the universal human truth that persuasion and motivation are driven by emotions can change everything about how you approach product development, marketing, employee engagement and customer experience. However, discovering truths—beliefs and feelings—is not all that simple because they are hidden in the human mind. We are not fully aware of why we do what we do, and you cannot simply ask questions to reveal how people really think and feel or to explain their behaviors. We must not rely on what people say, and algorithms do not reveal the whys of human behavior. It is imperative to get into people's heads to reveal what truly motivates them, drives their behaviors and decisions. You have to change the way you think about how people think and shift your mental model from the "voice of the customer" to the "mind of the customer."

Hidden truths inspire insights that help you to rethink everything, challenge assumptions and chase down suspicions about why customers do what they do. But hidden truths live outside of our immediate awareness, and well beyond what conventional research techniques can reveal. That's why it is critical to stop settling for research data and start insisting on insights. Conventional research approaches simply cannot provide the deep insights necessary to understand what represents an emotionally resonant customer experience.

You have to spend time with customers, immerse yourself in their lives and live through product and brand experiences alongside them to fully understand their needs and desires. This is what we often refer to as the idea that marketing teams, innovation and customer experience managers must become "method marketers" in the same way method actors strive to become their characters. You have to walk a mile in the customer's shoes, even if they don't fit. Generating new products or improved customer experiences rarely happens in the office without first seeing and understanding why customers get up in the morning and how they live their lives every day.

CHAPTER 15

How to Put the Care in Health Care

BEING ADMITTED TO A HOSPITAL HAS TO BE THE MOST CRITICAL of all situations in which positive touchpoints matter. There's nothing pleasant about the experience. At the very least it induces high anxiety. At the very worst it can involve acute fear and the real possibility of a lot of pain. And at its very best it can induce relief and gratitude.

Nobody understands this better than Bob Riney, president and chief operating officer of Henry Ford Health System ("HFHS") in Detroit, Michigan. Bob has been at Henry Ford all thirty-three years of his working life. He has had the experience of working in every department in what has become a vast medical complex of hospitals, clinics and pharmacies. This kind of job longevity might lead some people to a kind of complacency, but in Bob's case, I sense he finds it just as exciting and full of inspiration and reinvention as he probably did starting fresh out of college.

When Henry Ford built his first namesake establishment in 1913, he said two things that forever guide its mission and subsequent quest: He saw a great hospital for the common man, but rather than just a hospital, he wanted to go one better; he wanted "a hotel for sick people." If Bob doesn't have these intentions pinned on his office wall, he certainly has them pinned in his mind.

Patients are not exactly customers. They do not come to you willingly, and facing illness is obviously different from customers buying shoes or vision robotics or an airline ticket. The experience of a hospital is so much more personal and dramatic than the experience of what we normally think of as a "brand," which makes the touchpoints of that experience all the more critical, and I don't think all hospitals see their importance as clearly or with the same conviction as Bob and the HFHS team. To them, the very nature of their "business" breeds a natural culture of caring deeply about both big and little things as seen through the eyes of patients, and Bob speaks of both with obvious tenderness.

A LITTLE BIG THING

Hospital stories are dramatic stories. Some patients in palliative care who know they are dying want to continue to communicate with family and friends near and far. They have neither the means nor access to the use of a computer, so the staff makes sure they get an iPad on loan. This is obviously a kind and thoughtful gesture, but it's only a fraction of the story.

Says Bob, "Instead of our IT person giving the iPad to a nurse and the nurse giving it to the patient, we have the IT person do it. We have them interact with the patient because they understand the impact of what they're doing with what we're doing as a hospital. I've had some of them who never go into our hospital come back to me and say this was their greatest work experience."

Talk about a touchpoint! Talk about story do! Talk about the little things you do mean so much more than the big things you say! This says it all in spades, and it's only one of a million story dos in this big-city healthcare complex.

"I WANT TO SEE MY GRANDCHILD"

Try to imagine dealing with a woman who is dying with only two or three days left to live. Almost by reflex you might ask if there is anything you can do for her with the expectation that she would want another blanket or a glass of water.

When a nurse in one of the Henry Ford community hospitals asked that question, the patient said, "I want to see my grandchild." At first the nurse did not quite understand, but she inquired a little more and found out that the woman's daughter was pregnant and she was about to become a first-time grandmother to a child she knew she would never see. The nurse found out further that the daughter lived about three hours away, and she arranged for the daughter to come for a visit. She also sought the collaboration of a medical technician to do something extraordinary: *they put the daughter in a bed next to her mother and hooked up an ultrasound machine so that the dying woman's request to "see" her grandchild could literally be met!* The fact that they did this unusual kindness on their own time should come as no surprise. The woman died the next day. Her daughter said nobody could have given her or her mother a greater gift.

Bob says, "There's no way you can write a policy about such things. The nurse and the ultrasound tech did not have to seek reams of official permission. The nurse came up with the idea and got the go-ahead from the doctors and just made it happen. It's the kind of story we spread throughout the organization via what I call my weekly huddle message as a reminder of the active, living story that is our ingrained culture of 'patient first.' And spreading the word just doesn't come from me. Each of our hospitals keeps an eye out for similar stories to share as iconic examples of the real meaning of patient care. It's better than any lecture from me." This is one of the more touching examples in this book about how great brands spread good-news of story doing as inspiration for all. It is the literal meaning of a peak end moment that matters most.

TELLING IT LIKE IT IS

The stories are also used as orientation for new people coming on board to graphically demonstrate what is expected of them, what they might expect of themselves and as inspiration for how they can connect emotionally to the work. They drive home the point that working in healthcare in any capacity is a calling, not a job.

The HFHS team is also not afraid to broadcast internal stories of things that do not go so well. One example tells of poor patient hand-off between specialists involving the death of a very well-known and beloved person in the Detroit community. There was no question of malpractice. The clinical outcome would not have changed, but the system broadcast it to demonstrate an example of the deleterious effect of poor communication. They even got the patient's widow to participate in the making of a video that showed patient care through the eyes of a patient and the patient's family.

Bob shared, "The video demonstrates in a very powerful way the stress level we caused for this patient and this family at the end of a life through poor internal communication. It's an example of how we try to get to our people on an emotional level about what we do wrong as well as what we do right. We make it very real, not in a punitive way, but in the spirit of learning and continuous improvement. And I think it says something about the effectiveness of transparency in broadcasting our stories that the positives by far outnumber the negatives. We set the expectations and then just let things flourish in their own way facility by facility. You can't make people care by executive order, but you might just make them see the light with dramatic stories."

I hope you find this initiative to be as extraordinary as I do. It's one thing to announce the recall of a brand for defects, but you can't recall a life, and an admission of any kind of culpability in the case of a death is quite amazing.

FOR GOODNESS SAKE, INNOVATE

It seems to me that while healthcare cries out for innovation, it does not get its fair share of that precious stuff. This is why it's good to see it is an important initiative at Henry Ford. That last little story, for example, illustrates an innovation in transparency. If companies cringe at getting attention for mistakes, it must be doubly difficult for a hospital. The effort here is intended as a concerted effort to reduce unintended patient harm with a no-excuses, zero-defect approach to patient-care outcomes.

Bob and other HFHS leaders promote entrepreneurial initiatives like this throughout the entire healthcare delivery system—in research work, in its Health Alliance Plan, home health services, and a, best-in-class Perfect Depression Program designed to address the prevalence of chronic depression. Their new Bloomfield Hills hospital was built from scratch with active involvement from the community and features an innovative design that gives it a Main Street feel. There's a Culinary Wellness program to help curb obesity. And in the best branding tradition, Home Health Services, Pharmacy Advantage and OptimEyes optometry care give the HFHS group a significant retail presence that helps to build brand visibility and recognition.

A LITTLE CONTEXT

Bob speaks of the Henry Ford Health System as part of the fabric of the community in which it functions. He expresses heartfelt feelings for Detroit with both vision and sympathy. Contrary to what we read and see on the daily news, Bob believes what goes down has every reason to go up and declares real optimism for a better future in Detroit. Businesses will always recognize a bargain, particularly when that bargain is chock full of talent ready and willing to go to work. Bob is convinced the rejuvenation and revitalization process is already under way in Detroit.

IT'S A HEALTH SYSTEM WITH ATTITUDE

"We operate in one of the richest *and* the poorest areas of the country," Bob explains. "Our patients go from very wealthy to others whose address could be under the viaduct, which means there is always the problem of reimbursement uncertainty. This tale of two cities demands incredible involvement from our people with discretionary effort, a willingness to go above and beyond the expected. I think their extra effort undoubtedly comes from both living and working in what has been a troubled social and economic environment. There has been a real need to help your neighbor, and this gets combined with a work culture of 'do the right thing.' It's an attitude of everybody pitching in."

STAYING POWER

Staying in one place for thirty-five years as Bob has can actually be harder than moving around every three or four years the way many execs do. Moving gives you a chance to hit the delete button on your track record just as if you were moving your house—you just toss out the old stuff. Staying put, however, everybody knows your track record and whether what you stand for has withstood the test in good times and bad.

Among typical senior managers, Bob has a unique perspective of his commitment to doing the right thing. As he shared, "There is so much out there that suggests that everything from work to relationships is transient in four- or five-year cycles, and I think there is a different story to be told, particularly to young people, about the value of staying the course so that you find change and grow within yourself rather than from anything external. I am not the person I was even five years ago. Change in current circumstance does not necessarily have to lead to abandonment or surrender; rather, it can be an opportunity for growth and reinvention. I think this is often the challenge of leadership and inevitable crises of the kind we face in our community. And by related circumstance, in our mission to deliver effective health care. I cannot see myself giving up this challenge for the sake of something new."

A UNIQUE VIEW OF LEADERSHIP

Over the years Bob has also developed a unique philosophy of leadership. He puts it this way: "Organizations have to remind themselves that there is a finite amount of energy, and the only thing we control about that energy is how we spend it. There are so many things that can come along to take people's energy away or turn it negative, which is why I look upon leadership as a kind of refueling station. I think a big part of the leader's job is to help refuel energy, not by being a cheerleader or a Pollyanna, but by listening, by responding, by always creating context and standing up to owning decisions whether they be positive or negative. No leader gets a free pass on any of that."

Of all the possible perspectives on leadership (and there a million of them out there) I think Bob's is perhaps the most thoughtful and original I have ever heard. It leads me to believe that he would be a great boss to work for. Bob sees that leadership is all about *human truths* that guide an organization to success or failure. He supports my belief that success is all about sorting out the wheat from the chaff of what is truly important and focusing on the things that fuel an organization and its people's energy for doing the right thing.

In one of the *Godfather* movies, Michael Corleone says to his brother, "It's not personal, Sonny. It's business." Well, Michael got that one very wrong. All business is personal. There is no such thing as any kind of contract that goes without the social imperative of trust, of giving and receiving full measure, and the assurance of satisfaction delivered in good time and good faith. You would not seek medical care that delivered any less, just as you would not suffer less from a brand you buy from a store. If you doubt any of this, I might just sic Bob Riney on you for a lesson in timeless wisdom.

Henry Ford Health Services delivers all of the essentials that I think drive any successful company. Its people focus on the things that matter, and they create positive experiences around them. Its leaders conduct regular dialogue with staff. They listen, as well as talk and take action on the feedback they get. The staff is engaged with customers and encouraged to show genuine affection when meeting customers' needs. Everybody takes guidance from a higher-order mission and makes it not just a work quest, but the active story of a life quest.

It is worthwhile to note that these decidedly human attitudes for success do not cost more than any other kind of attitudes. Actually, doing the right thing costs a lot less when you factor in the employee engagement and retention created from being part of something that matters. Add to it that those committed employees contribute more than anything else to foster patient satisfaction and loyalty. It all adds up to the unbeatable focused energy that drives success and return on investment that is truly remarkable in every way. Bob Riney and Henry Ford Health Services obviously have large doses of both.

INSIGHT—YOU MUST DECIDE TO MANAGE OR TO LEAD

The difference between managers and leaders is night and day. Managers are trained to deal with things. Leaders are compelled to change things. When organizations face daunting challenges, managers try to optimize operations to absorb the problems. Leaders recognize what is at the heart of the challenge and transform the organization to focus on what really matters. Organizations with competent managers can navigate and survive challenges. Organizations facing even the most daunting situations can *thrive* when they have courageous leaders who focus all their energies on changing the game.

Running a group of hospitals is an enormous challenge. Running a hospital in the midst of all the issues facing Detroit could be viewed as insurmountable. Such an enormous challenge can be a rich source of easy excuses; it's just not possible to overcome all these problems. Yet, when leaders clearly focus and pour their energies into the right things, it inspires everyone around them to accomplish what never seemed possible. Inspiration is the most powerful tool any leader can wield. Managers manage. But a leader has the mandate and seizes the obligation to inspire her people and her customers. An organization facing difficult challenges can overcome and thrive if its leadership is willing to rise above the fray and embrace the greater quest. When organizations don't succeed it is because leadership simply fails to identify and devote their energies to what matters most. As is so truly stated, "The buck stops here."

CHAPTER 16

Experience is Everything

HOSPITALS SHARE TWO THINGS IN COMMON WITH HOTELS: BOTH usually get the opportunity to live with their customers for more than casual periods of time, and both get the chance to deliver unprecedented levels of intimate, hands-on customer care. The Body Holiday in Saint Lucia gives us an unusual example of a resort hotel that delivers all of the above.

The island itself has been called the Jewel of the Caribbean, and indeed, it is an island the way an island was meant to be in your most vivid imagination. But a sparkling location is only a small part of why The Body Holiday is one of the unusual stories in Caribbean tourism. It enjoys the distinction of being fully occupied all year because of the intense emotional content of a remarkably different vacation experience.

The hotel is owned by the Barnard family and was put in the hands of hotelier member, Craig Barnard, when it was acquired in 1978. It was bought for its picture-postcard location on a virtually private quarter-moon of white-sand beach, but Craig saw much more than the standard holiday offering.

The difference between brand "story doing" and "story telling" was not on the radar when the Body Holiday was conceived, but Craig instinctively saw story doing as the way to go, and he enlisted the help of two marketing people who had invented very active and very different resort concepts in Jamaica, namely Couples (the first of its kind for couples only) and its counterpoint, Hedonism (dedicated to the idea that being a little wicked is the best revenge). One was George Whitfield, and in the spirit of full disclosure, the other was our very own coauthor of this book, Harrison Yates.

Craig had an idea that a comprehensive spa experience combined with all the benefits of a luxurious and first-class beach resort might bring a new and unique kind of experience to the Caribbean—one that filled a need for the growing search among baby boomers for better health and well-being mixed in with the hedonistic desire for sea, sun and sand.

There were a few good dedicated spas in Europe, and even one or two in the American west, but they tended to be rigid examples of diet restriction and mandated physical activity mixed in with various kinds of massage and water treatments that hardly seem compatible with the word "vacation." As one of the team members said, "I'm surprised these places don't require you to wear a hair shirt and take a vow of silence."

DO AS YOU PLEASE, PLEASE

Craig and his team spent considerable time working out the salient touchpoints of the experience and, to this day, it still remains unique not only in the Caribbean, but in the entire world. The most important feature turned out to be the opportunity for each guest to custom design the holiday of his or her own choosing. "It's your holiday, not ours, and we never forget it" was one of the driving mantras. Do you want to fill your days with vigorous exercise in the form of tennis, golf, fencing, archery, sailing, snorkeling, scuba diving, pool and beach volley ball, rain forest hikes, tai chi, gymnasium workouts, Pilates and more—all with expert instruction as much as you require? Or do you want to find your own bliss in the form of many different kinds of exotic massage and special baths given to you with the laying on of discreet, expert hands? And by the way, one hour of these body treats comes free of charge daily in a beautiful and tranquil wellness center that is a healing oasis in its own right.

Or maybe your wife wants the spa and you want the sports. Or maybe one of you wants the whole shebang and the other wants to loll on the beach or by one of the three pools, giving up on any kind of attempt at a diet by indulging one's appetite for hedonistic food in one of four indulgent restaurants.

The first option obviously requires a bit of planning and scheduling, but you can pick and choose and set it all up even before you arrive. This was always an option from day one made even easier with the advent of the Internet.

POCKETS NOT REQUIRED

The resort avoids the label of "all-inclusive" simply because it smacks of downscale, which is never an adjective anyone would use to describe the evident luxury and esthetic charm of The Body Holiday; rather, Craig simply sees the fact that most of what is available is offered on a complimentary basis as a matter of convenience and an escape from ever thinking about what things cost on your precious vacation time. This little thing is appreciated by the largely international clientele who value this unique touchpoint as a moment of escape from carrying anything in their pockets beyond a room key. Especially since they were probably nickel and dimed to death by an airline on their way to St. Lucia with extra charges for bags, seats with legroom, drinks, wireless and anything else most airlines can think of.

Craig also sees the idea that quite literally, there's no charge for that, as a matter of good manners. He puts it this way: "I would not invite you to my house and expect you to pay me for cocktails, wine or dinner. And why on earth would you consider leaving me a tip?" As a result, only the more exotic discretionary treatments come with any kind of charge beyond what you pay your travel agent.

A QUEST TO LIVE BY

The team thought long and hard about the name and the inherent quest that would fulfill the promise of self-chosen wellness in body and mind. What they came up with tells the story with vivid presence that both the staff and the brand's customers can internalize with passion and conviction. It's a provocative, highly-involved proposition that says, "Give us your body for a week and we'll give you back your mind."

This is the brand's North Star, very much like the IBM line I often quote as a North Star example: "Let's make a smarter planet." And indeed, "Give us your body for a week and we'll give you back your mind" is not only the driving brand quest, but it's also the headline that has adorned *every* ad the resort has ever run since 1995!

THE HOLIDAY THAT GOES HOME WITH YOU

The team also recognized that while each guest can customize his or her own holiday experience, those who choose to pursue the exercise and spa options garner skills and insights that last long after their tans have faded. While the conventional beach resort will leave you with pleasant memories and a few good Facebook moments, going to The Body Holiday is a bit like learning to ride a bicycle: once you learn something like how to meditate for the achievement of inner peace, you never forget it. Same for yoga and Tai Chi or the tips you pick up from the golf and tennis pros. Or customized dietary advice available to all guests that might forever change your eating habits.

These are among the many skills you can acquire and call on when the events of work and generally managing life back home leave you feeling up to your knees in alligators of stress that can put your natural body-mind rhythm out of whack. And this puts The Body Holiday firmly in the camp of brands that don't just *tell* a good story; they *do* it.

Craig and team did not read a book like this that inspired them to "dream up" a higher-values purpose for their enterprise. Their instincts led them naturally to believe they should *actually* deliver the unique experience they promised. They also did not think they were making tourism history, but a former manager of the hotel told Harrison that The Body Holiday story is used as a case history at the Cornell University School of Hotel Management, and little did they dream that Conde Nast Traveler magazine would in 2013 vote The Body Holiday the *#1 destination spa in the world.*

The Body Holiday name evolved as a natural extension of the brand promise, and it falls into the best tradition of very different brand names modern startups now adopt to communicate the active essence, function and role they intend to play in their customers' lives. As Jim Stengel says in *Grow,* "If you are not ambitious enough to want to make a big difference in people's lives, you won't make a positive difference in your business. Ideals move millions, along with politics, war, peace, art, science, and maybe mountains." The thought here is "go big or go home." The world does not need another nice little hotel on the beach where you can get a tan. There are thousands of them already out there lining beaches all over the globe. People deserve an *involving experience* along with their hard-earned sunburns, and that is what they get when they choose The Body Holiday. "Give us your body for a week and we'll give you back your mind" is not the ad campaign for this year. It is the driving force behind the brand's ambitious purpose. Craig protects it with the zeal of a red-coated British Army Guardsman at Buckingham Palace where he went to receive his Member of the British Empire honor from Queen Elizabeth a few years ago.

DON'T FORGET THE WORKERS

By the very nature of its function as both a luxury hotel and full-service spa, The Body Holiday has a high staff-to-guest ratio, and it is instilled into every staff member that they are an essential part of the holiday. They are not passive servants. They are on the front line of all that goes on, and they are taught that their behavior can make or break the way a guest feels about the total experience. This includes everybody from housekeeping to gardeners to the guy who certifies you for scuba diving and the masseuse whose hands transport you to heavenly bliss. This is an intimate resort (no more than 120 rooms) that guests take very personally.

While most people come as a couple, singles are made to feel at home with a special room rate, and well-trained "Body Guards" make sure they are never made to feel like outsiders. The Body Guards (male and female) are social hosts who might stop by your breakfast table with an invitation to the afternoon beach volleyball match between staff and guests. They are not the "rah-rah" merchants you find in a lot of cruise ships; rather, they are discrete facilitators ready and willing to help guests get the most out of the experience. They are more like a band of fun-loving concierges who live by the credo that nothing you want is ever a problem.

These socially adept people exemplify my conviction that there is a strong correlation between employee attitude and a brand's financial performance. Hotel margins are notoriously slim, but when you fill your facility with people coming back for more year after year, you are bound to do very well. For one thing, it costs a great deal less to entice returns from loyal customers than to recruit new ones. As willing brand ambassadors, these customers are the brand's most important asset, and the resort sees them as essential purveyors of the customer experience when they return home.

IF YOU'RE GOOD, GET BETTER

Heir apparent Andrew Barnard is both marketing director and deputy CEO, and he has lived with a deep-seated understanding of the brand's culture since childhood. The tradition of never being quite satisfied is one he feels as deeply as his father, and many millions of dollars have been spent to enhance both the physical surroundings and the content of the experience over the years.

Andrew proudly explains, "We do not go along with the idea of 'if it ain't broke, don't fix it.' It's our job to listen to what our guests want, and to even anticipate their needs before they voice them. We started out with two restaurants. Now we have four and we get super-high marks for the dining experience, both in variety of choice and excellence of preparation—so much so that dedicated gourmets could come for the food alone. We keep adding new exotic treatments at the Wellness Centre and have Master Classes with world authorities we invite to teach and give counsel on various wellness disciplines during the summer months. We now offer beauty treatments like Botox enhancement for those who request it. It goes on and on and will do so forever. Standing still is never an option. I think some guests even come back every year to see what we have done to the place!"

This process of listening and responding to what is heard is the mark of all great brands. And it returns expected dividends. Guests appreciate being met at the airport and getting transportation provided to the hotel.

They like not having a front desk; rather, when they get to the hotel they are invited into a comfortable lounge and offered a cold drink after their journey while they fill out their short registration form. If they do not want to be bothered with it on arrival, they can take it to their room and do it later. Highly attentive receptionists sit casually at desks and guests take a seat when speaking to them rather than standing at a counter. Your luggage is whisked away on your arrival and is magically there when you get to your room, which is beautifully furnished with a king-sized four-poster bed and usually an ocean view from an inviting balcony. A ritual afternoon tea is elegantly served in the spacious, open-to-the-sea clubhouse at the end of every day with a background of classical music softly playing as the falling sun paints the sky with its gaudy brush. Guests like it that one of the restaurants is casual about what you wear at dinner, that the piano bar doesn't close until the last guest goes to bed, and that there is hardly a moment during the day and evening when you can't get something very good to eat

If all of this sounds idyllic, it is idyllic on purpose. A famous designer once said that God is in the details. Details by their very nature are always little. At The Body Holiday the details of each day form the important little touchpoints of the experience that create rave reviews and an unprecedented number of guests who return year after year. Multiplying detail after experiential detail is simply part of the team's culture. It doesn't cost more to be considerate of how even little things contribute to the customer's experience and how it makes them feel. The Barnards see it as investment rather than cost. "We are a customer culture, not a cost culture. When you command a premium price, you can't afford *not* to do more and more" is Craig's answer to the question. It's an answer, by the way, that justifies the thrust of this book: the little things you do, the human things, don't cost more, and those things easily pay for themselves with the high returns earned as a result customer satisfaction, loyalty and advocacy.

THE FUTURE IS RIGHT NOW

While The Body Holiday was indeed ahead of its time creating an extraordinary customer experience coming out of a quest of a very high order, it is now what new brands in any field aim for from the brand's very beginnings. Michael Wilkings, a wise and engaging man in the hospitality field who runs a company called Leisure Resources Group, puts it well in one of his quarterly newsletters: "Impeccable service is now the norm. Anything less becomes the subject of comment ... well-traveled consumers today are seeking experiences, emotional connections that excite and linger longer than normal. Customers want to feel an emotional response from a server or resort concierge. A mechanically perfect job is never enough. The hospitality professional must put his or her heart into giving the customer an experience to remember."

He could easily be describing The Body Holiday's philosophy and modus operandi. He could also be describing how many of today's intriguing startups plan to dominate the businesses of tomorrow.

How could The Body Holiday spread its standout reputation around the world? Could Craig and Andrew export their resort experience to other exotic locations? Could they generate big buzz by opening mini Body Holidays in major city centers? Could they sponsor experiential events the way a story-doing brand like Red Bull does? Could they create a health and wellness blog featuring the latest news and science for healthy living? Could they make their brand of bliss portable by transporting the experience to cold weather destinations like world class ski resorts where a deep-tissue massage for tired muscles delivered in spontaneous, quick-hit, pop-up venues might be seen as a memorable moment? They could, indeed, as long as they preserve the brand's quest to provide experiences that fulfill whatever matters most to customers.

The best thing about the future is that it lasts a long time and great brands never stand still in it. I have a feeling the future will be seeing a lot of The Body Holiday. The brand got its start with gutsy innovation by creating a customer experience that did not exist until Craig and his slightly nutty but highly inventive fellow conspirators were inspired to do it. The brand has been rewarded with countless customer smiles, incredible stories of rejuvenation and a repeat guest ratio that rivals any resort anywhere. You could also say, "Give us your body for a week and you'll give it to us for many more weeks to come." This habit of creating extraordinary customer experiences is one we can be thankful The Body Holiday team will not soon break.

INSIGHT—IT IS THE CUSTOMER'S EXPERIENCE THAT MATTERS, NOT YOURS

In the midst of the daily stress and strife of managing a business, it's easy to fall into the trap of focusing more on your experience than the customer's. It's almost forgivable because you have to identify and address a lot of things that your customers don't see and are hopefully never aware of. Yet, what matters most is how the experience of your brand makes employees feel and, in turn, how it makes your customers feel and how they choose to share your brand story with their friends. The fact is the experience you must understand and provide is theirs, not yours. When you lose sight of this reality or neglect to put yourself in your employees' and customer's shoes, your chances plummet for realizing the kind of success you imagined. Your brand won't break through the clutter, won't deliver experiences that create loyal employees and customers and is unlikely to produce the sustainable financial results you desire. Whatever management thinks matters very little beyond how your employees and customers experience and feel about it.

CHAPTER 17

Rallying 'Round the Flag

OUT OF ALL THE LEADERSHIP STORIES THAT INSPIRE EMPLOYEE empowerment I share in this book, the most unusual of them all has to be one from the U.S. Navy. Military service may strike you as a classic environment for top-down command and control leadership of the most regimented kind. Unfailing obedience is a necessity for men and women required to put their lives on the line. It would hardly seem to include the listening and questioning model required for enlightened leadership. Doing things by the book is *de rigueur.* It's shape up or ship out. If it moves, salute it; if it doesn't move, paint it. Ours is not to reason why; ours is but to do or die. There's the right way, the wrong way, and the navy way. No questions asked as you go over the top, boys and girls. And remember that it wasn't too many years ago when sailors were pressed into service—literally kidnapped and hauled aboard to serve what must have felt like a criminal sentence as they were tied to the rigging and flogged with a cat-o'-nine-tails for minor rule infractions. It's hardly the ideal environment for what Peter Drucker called "systematic innovation."

AN OFFICER AND A GENTLEMAN

That's what so impressive about the story of Commander D. Michael Abrashoff, once captain of a formidable $1 billion warship, armed with the world's most advanced and lethal computer-controlled combat system. His remarkable story was first brought to my attention when reported by Polly LaBarre in *Fast Company* magazine. She writes that Comdr. Abrashoff is a model of leadership that is as progressive as any in the business world. But it's precisely because he was in the military that I find the commander's story even more remarkable.

The 28-year-old Abrashoff had a sterling service record, including combat experience, but it's his ship and her crew that he talks about with unabashed pride. When he took command, The *Benfold* was classified as one of the worst ships in the Navy. When he got through with it, it was credited with the best record in the Pacific fleet for combat readiness. To keep it that way, he saw his mission as "nothing less than the reorientation of a famously rigid 200-year-old hierarchy." His aim: to focus on *purpose* rather than chain of command. "When you shift your organizing principle from obedience to performance," said Abrashoff, "the highest boss is no longer the guy with the most stripes—it's the sailor who does the work. There's nothing magical about it … In most organizations today, ideas still come from the top. Soon after arriving at this command I realized that the young folks on this ship were smart and talented. And I realized that my job was to listen aggressively—to pick up all of the ideas that they had for improving how we operate."

BELIEVERS AND INFIDELS

Abrashoff truly thinks "the most important thing a captain can do is to see the ship from the eyes of its crew." He further believes that there's always a better way to do things, and he probed those better ways in great detail with the crew. He and his crew dissected every operation to see how each one helped them to maintain operational readiness. There was no reticence about making stunning changes that seem highly unusual for a military organization. Anything and everything that was done just because "that's the way we always do things" was jettisoned overboard. In his mission to create true operational readiness, Abrashoff pursued a policy of what in branding terms might be called "organizational abandonment."

Many of his superiors and fellow commanding officers questioned Abrashoff's methods. He says, "I divide the world into believers and infidels. What the infidels don't understand—and they far outnumber the believers—is that innovative practices combined with true empowerment produce phenomenal results."

One of his confident insights into change is that the more people enjoy the process, the better the results. Spending thirty-five days in the Persian Gulf is no fun for a crew of very young people, but during replenishment alongside supply ships, the *Benfold*'s crew was known throughout the region for projecting music videos on another ship's side. In purchasing food for the ship, Abrashoff switched from high-cost naval provisions to cheaper, better-quality, name-brand foods. With the money he saved, he sent five of the *Benfold's* thirteen cooks to cooking school, which made the *Benfold* a favorite lunchtime destination for crews across the San Diego waterfront. Abrashoff's ship had a $2.4 million maintenance budget and a $3 million repair budget. He was able to return $1.4 million of these amounts to the navy's bottom line, which he credits to a proactive environment in which people simply want to do well.

ONE LITTLE THING AFTER ANOTHER

On average, only 54 percent of sailors remain in the navy after their second tour of duty. Under Abrashoff's command, 100 percent of the *Benfold's* career sailors signed on for another tour. He figures this saved $1.6 million in costs related to personnel. He understood that scraping and chipping paint was a hated chore and a waste of the crew's time and talent. He farmed the job out and incalculably boosted morale, while increasing sailors' time for training and combat readiness (it also got the ship a paint job that lasts thirty years for a mere $25,000). On his watch, the *Benfold's* sailors came out winners in the advancement cycle, with promotions twice as high as the Navy average.

He created an Internet account so that the sailors on sea duty could send and get messages home daily through a commercial satellite. When new crewmembers arrived fresh from boot camp, they were greeted with a welcome plan, which included a hand-picked mentor and the right to call home to let the folks know they had arrived safely (Abrashoff paid for the call). He made sure he knew every crewmember through face-to-face meetings and understood his or her goals. Needless to say, he remembered every person's name.

When he learned that credit-card debt was causing serious trouble for many of the young crew, he hired financial consultants to provide advice. He broadcast new ideas over the ship's loudspeakers. Sailors made a suggestion one week and saw it implemented the next.

Abrashoff says, "None of this means we sacrificed discipline or cohesion on the ship. When I walked down the passageway, people called 'Attention on deck' and hit the bulkhead. They respected the office, but also understood I don't care about the fluff—I want substance. And the substance is combat readiness. The substance is having people feel good about what they do. The substance is treating people with respect and dignity. We gained a lot of ground by keeping our focus on substance rather than on a lot of extraneous stuff."

The examples and sterling results of Abrashoff's intense-listening command style go on and on. They would indeed create envy in the best leaders in business today. He says, "In many units—and in many businesses—a lot of time and effort is spent supporting the guy on top. Anyone on my ship will tell you that I'm a low-maintenance CO. It's not about me, it's about my crew."

THE CAPTAIN TELLS ALL

Abrashoff revealed his perspective on leadership that made the Benfold experience such a shining example of what can happen when leaders have an enlightened sense of what it means to lead:

- Don't just take command, communicate purpose.
- Leaders listen without prejudice.
- Practice discipline without formalism.
- The best captains hand out responsibility, not orders.
- Successful crews perform with devotion.
- True change is permanent: once you start perestroika, you can't really stop it.

I would like to see these principles engraved in stone and hung on the wall of every CEO's office. If no other leadership principles were presented in this or any other book, Commander Abrashoff's would be enough.

He also says, "I'm lucky. All I ever wanted to do in the Navy was to command a ship. I didn't care if I ever got promoted again. And that attitude enabled me to do the right things for my people instead of doing the right things for my career. In the process, I ended up with the best ship in the Navy—and I got the best evaluation of my career." After completing his 20-month tour of duty on the Benfold,

Commander Abrashoff reported to a top post at the Space and Naval Warfare Systems Command. He has since left the Navy and successfully writes and lectures on the subject of leadership.

The lesson is that empowerment is one of leadership's primary goals. You don't hire people so you can tell them what to do. You hire people so you never have to tell them what to do. Leadership is what happens when you are not there. As the leader, you are needed for keeping the faith, for making final decisions, for leadership in emergencies and for plotting the future of your business or brand.

You might also be needed for playing the trombone in the company band. It's a good idea to remind yourself that you are not Vladimir Putin and your company isn't Russia. When you enter the boardroom, you do not have to change from the person you are with friends and family to the instant tough-guy executive. You don't treat people as you want to treat them; you treat them the way they want to be treated. Everyone is an individual with a desire to be part of something meaningful and you take that little fact into account in helping him or her figure out how to make a worthwhile contribution.

I find it's also useful, as did Abrashoff, to shift your perspective on who's there to serve whom. I like to think of myself as a servant leader whose job is to serve my team, not the other way around. Very simply, people want to work for—and do business with—people they can respect and admire, who espouse leadership from carefully constructed principles and values.

We can get it very right when we absorb the beautifully expressed advice of Mary Parker Follet who once wrote, "The leader guides the group and is at the same time guided by the group, is always part of the group … Authority, genuine authority, is the outcome of our common life. It does not come from separating people, from dividing them into two classes: those who command and those who obey. It comes from the intermingling of all, of my work fitting into yours and yours into mine."

Amen to that!

INSIGHT—TRUE ENGAGEMENT MUST BE CAUGHT, NOT TAUGHT.

There is a familiar refrain from what we hear in all the examples of successful leaders and great companies in this book—the most effective way to transform an organization is to inspire its stakeholders with *shared* purpose and meaning. Shared purpose can only occur when leaders communicate openly and listen to their colleagues with an appreciative ear. True engagement will only occur when it is caught, not taught. It's most contagious form is a responsive action from a trusted leader. It's most destructive form is an inauthentic leader's inattention.

By its very nature, shared purpose trickles down and bubbles up in a fully motivated and engaged organization. Incredible returns are achieved by sharing responsibility, not by handing down orders from on high. The discipline and accountability to do the right thing for customers cannot be achieved unless everyone understands and embraces his or her critical role and assumes his or her responsibility.

CHAPTER 18

The Big Miracle for Little Mortals

IN THE WORST NEIGHBORHOODS OF CHICAGO, ONE WOMAN'S mission is literally changing the lives of hundreds of children who might very well be doomed to die in a gang war, grow up to go to prison, suffer from drug addiction or remain forever in the poverty and misery that perpetuate the tragedy of broken lives.

I know this story well; the woman in question is Donnita Travis. She is my wife. My pride in her is only superseded by the consequences of her truly incredible achievements. But that's not why I tell her story here. I tell it because all great nonprofit brands have something they can teach everybody managing a for-profit brand about the motivating power of a quest for heroic cause and the bewitching allure of no-holds-barred, over-the-top customer service and experiential involvement.

EVEN A TERRIBLE DAY IS A GOOD DAY TO START REBUILDING LIVES

On the infamous day of September 11, 2001, an after-school program started its first day in a once-abandoned space in the notorious Chicago housing project known as Cabrini Green. It was the beginning of a truly amazing organization called By The Hand Club.

Forty-two children attended that fateful day. That same after-school program has grown to serve 1,000 kids in four of Chicago's most under-resourced neighborhoods. From just a handful of volunteers there are now 300 with hundreds more sought in anticipation of the avalanche of new kids banging the doors down to get in—doors, by the way, that are open until 7:30 in the evening.

HOW TO FILL AN EMPTY HOLE

We all have too much stuff and we're presented with more of it every day. I sometimes wonder how the floors in the average American house can bear the weight of all the stuff we cart home. Old Mother Hubbard's cupboard had a problem with scarcity. Today it would be filled with a dozen different varieties of breakfast cereal and a half-dozen different brands or flavors of canned spaghetti sauce.

That's why new brands can only be successful today when they offer something new and different in the form of a social, as well as an economic, quest. Products like Honest Tea are conceived to fill the need for a tasty bottled drink that was full of refreshing but healthier calories. Twitter filled a social gap not served by Facebook. Tesla might succeed in the tough marketplace on luxury cars only because it offers a new, different kind of automobile, and magazines like Consumer Report classify it as the best car they have ever tested.

In the same vein, By The Hand Club came along to help underprivileged children to feel safe at a critical time of day in their inner city lives. The safety of children might be thought of as a more noble cause than inventing a thirst quencher or another dot com or another way to clutter the world's highways, but the principle is the same: a me-too new brand in today's saturated marketplace has no reason to succeed. In By The Hand Club's case, the brand didn't fill a hole; it filled a chasm.

THE MOST DANGEROUS TIME

Families in Chicago housing projects like Cabrina Green are By The Hand Club's customers. They are never far from poverty and a fear of violence that is hard for the average American family to comprehend. For the kids, after school is when the violence is at its worst. That's when they face the reality that Chicago is the youth homicide capital of the U.S. Seventy-seven kids were killed during 2014 in Chicago, compared to forty-eight in L.A. and seventeen in New York. Plus, the kids might well come from broken homes or a home run by a mother struggling without help to survive. A large number of fathers are in prison. Drugs and addiction are everywhere. So are the street gangs fighting for turf and roosts to rule.

It is in these desolate neighborhoods where Donnita found her life's work. She gave up a successful advertising career in a chic downtown office tower for a job that takes her daily to the most dangerous parts of Chicago where even many cab drivers are afraid to go. The job pays exactly zero dollars but is rich in the spiritual reward that comes from unstinting service to others. You might say she swapped life in the fast lane for life in the love lane.

A NAME TO REMEMBER

A name like General Electric was conceived at a time when electricity was a new consumer force. If it were starting up today, it would probably be called something like Zap City. General Motors might be called Go-Go.com. The generic generals of yesterday are being replaced on company letterheads with welcome color and imagination.

Names today are more descriptive and involving than names ever were. Think of Twitter, Facebook, Buzzmamas, Threadless, skinnyCorp, Tumblr, Google, Reddit, Yahoo!, and all the other dot coms with highly active names that work hard to describe the sense and sensibility of their offerings with compelling contemporary metaphor.

By The Hand Club follows this prescription with a fabulously evocative and unforgettable name that brings the brand's mission to life with power and clarity. It says loving care, shelter from the storm, and the uncommon kindness and compassion of Christ's petition, "suffer the little children to come unto me." The word club doesn't sound like a boring old school, and By The Hand has in it a little of the feeling of the 23rd Psalm: "… Yea, though I walk through the valley of death I fear no evil, for thou art with me, thy rod and they staff they comfort me …" The fact that I think of it in biblical terms is entirely appropriate: Donnita found her inspiration in John 10:10, which reads: "The thief comes to steal, kill and destroy. But I've come that you may have life and have it more abundantly."

THE MISSION TO END ALL MISSIONS

As shown throughout this book, leaders, companies and brands are becoming more and more aware of the power of espousing a purpose that transcends the mere utility of their products. Even an ordinary household product like Dove soap does the same by trying to democratize beauty "to celebrate every woman's unique beauty." There are literally dozens and dozens of examples of successful new brands driven by higher-order purpose and a quest to contribute more to the world than a flush financial statement. These brands are eye-openers to those who have a practical, cold-blooded, self-serving view of business. But not to their loyal droves of customers who expect ... no, demand, more from modern businesses.

Because there is no commerce involved, all nonprofits have the ideal opportunity to adopt and inspire a higher purpose in the role they play in peoples' lives. Since By The Hand is faith-based and committed to knocking down the social and personal barriers that block children from learning, a clear, precise and involving statement of mission is paramount for the benefit of customers, staff, donors and all other constituents, even suppliers who influence the brand's success.

As By The Hand takes kids on the journey from first grade and walks them all the way through college, the brand's engraved-in-stone mission is:

To take kids in critical need for intervention by the hand
and lead them to a new and abundant life in body, mind
and soul.

Missions don't get any more ambitious than that, and this one does not need help from a slogan. The slogan is built into the name itself.

EMOTION WINS

Donnita's Northwestern University MBA and eighteen years of advertising management experience helped her take on By The Hand. With her experience in branding, she completely gets it that to keep satisfied customers and "shareholders" who donate the funds to keep the "business" going, she has to be accountable for tangible, documented evidence that By The Hand maintains its brand promise, that it's doing what it sets out to do for the present and future of its customers. To this end, By The Hand is often praised for complete transparency, innovative product research, sensitivity to data collection and return on investment in the form of the kids' success.

It's difficult to measure love, but these little customers account for it clearly in their responses. Donnita says, "If you asked the kids what we do best, I'm pretty sure they would say that we love them. And we really do."

She illustrates her point with a little story: "I was in the office with a student the other day and I said to him, 'I'm having a great day.' Then I looked at him and said, 'Guess why I'm having a great day?' He smiled and said, *'Because you got to see me?'* I thought my heart would burst. That one moment of affirmation with that one child is as important to me as great academic test results because building character and self-worth one-by-one are just as valuable as the collective numbers on a test score."

Another of her love stories involves a boy named Kevon: "At the end of every day, I would give Kevon a piece of candy and hug him and tell him I love him and I didn't think much about it. After a couple of months he was getting ready to go home and he said, 'Miss Donnita, you got a piece of candy?' I told him I was a bit busy and that Rochelle would give it to him. He said, 'No. I want *you* to give it to me.' It took me a while to figure out what he was saying but it dawned on me that what he was really asking for was, 'I want a hug. And I want to know you love me.'"

It's the little things that really matter that Donnita and her staff do day in and day out that mean just as much as getting the kids eyeglasses or a mattress to sleep on, and giving them a chance at a decent education. *All* these things are critical touchpoints that are the lifeblood of experiential brands. She says, "We can say we love them and tell them Jesus loves them, but without all the intangible little things, we would fail to reach the final goal. Mother Teresa said, 'It's not how much we give but how much love we put into giving'. And if you want to work with children Mother Theresa lights the way."

The emphasis on love is instinctive, but by no means accidental. My team at Brandtrust conducted deep-dive Emotional Inquiry research with the students to discover what really goes on in the minds of kids in distress. What we discovered is that they have to feel safe and secure physically and emotionally before they can ever think about learning. They have to go from the flight mode of basic survival to "Hey, I'm okay." That's where love comes in.

KEEPING SCORE

The hard-core numbers are impressive. Kids come to By The Hand Club not meeting reading standards. By The Hand delivers a 100 percent senior high school graduation rate with double and triple percentage increases in reading and math scores for Chicago Public School students. Kids who come to the school failing are now averaging a B-minus grade point average, 187 of them are on the honor roll, and 91 percent of graduates are going to college. This is an incredible turnaround from lives of unquiet desperation to lives of hope and possibility—even more impressive than a for-profit brand posting enviable numbers on its bottom line.

EXTRINSIC REWARDS, INTRINSIC MORALE

The brand does extensive networking to keep its profile high on the donor radar screen. A lot of the recognition for the brand's effectiveness goes to Donnita personally, which is important to her only for its ability to get donor-friendly ink for the brand in the press. She was named Chicagoan of the year for 2013. Chicago's former mayor, Richard M. Daley, gave her the SAGE award for her work with women and children in 2010. Northwestern University named her Social Entrepreneur of the Year, and she received a fellowship to go to Harvard.

She says, "It's good for staff and investors to feel we are doing well, but after all is said and done, I look to the kids for the ultimate confirmation of that, and I always want to do better, to be a better leader, to do more and more to lead our kids to successful lives. That's where I look first."

BRAND DISCIPLINES

All brands run on effective business practice as well as emotional connections. By The Hand is no different. It is run with all the rigor and best practices of a Fortune 500 brand.

Every staff member (including Donnita) has a personal development and performance plan. Each has a six-month goal to help them achieve the vision of the mission, and each person is reviewed for progress quarterly with his or her supervisor. As executive director, Donnita actually presents her personal development plan to the board of directors for feedback on how well she is doing. A child protection policy is strictly enforced and regular meetings are held with staff to review what By The Hand is doing right, what the organization is doing wrong and how it can be fixed. Communication between staff and management is always wide open. We see something similar in the brands featured in this book where open cultures embrace the ethic of speak your mind, don't do as you're told but do what's right, and do it in an accountable but personal fashion.

Even part-time volunteers go through background checks and get a day of "shadowing"—an orientation process where they learn about brand culture through exposure so they can decide whether they think they have what it takes to mentor kids. If they proceed, they are assigned the place where their particular strengths can be best put to use. Says Donnita, "The guiding hand for everybody is the welfare of the kids and the ever-present promise of abundant life. This dominates the culture. But I sometimes wonder who is getting the more abundant life out of this promise – the kids or the people who work for them!"

PARTY TIME

Healthy brand cultures don't need big excuses to celebrate. Cognex is a prime example of the cultural power of throwing a good party just for the heck of it. Southwest makes every one of its flights a celebration. Zappos's employees bring joy to work with them every day. Families and even countries share collective joy with anniversaries and national holidays.

For the kids at By The Hand, it's important to recognize that the eventual rewards of academic success are not what motivate them. These things are too far off in the future for them to appreciate. The best effect comes from rewards that are much more tangible and immediate. This is the case, at least, until they experience the intrinsic, self-directed value of success. As was learned from research, the touchpoints of extrinsic motivation and celebrating small successes and signals of progress in a tangible and more immediate way work wonders to keep the kids engaged.

To this end, the staff holds what are known as ABC parties for those who made As, Bs and Cs. To the kids, love is spelled T-I-M-E, so there are field trips and a variety of competitions and rewards associated with learning along with ever-present reminders of how much they are loved. Anybody who thinks back to his or her school days will recall moments when special attention from a teacher could make you feel a foot taller. Praise for a specific skill can often inspire a later career. For By The

Hand kids, it can inspire hope for a future. In the words of C.S. Lewis, "The proper aim of giving is to put the recipients in a state where they no longer need our gifts."

WATCHING OUT FOR RED TAPE CREEP

When an organization grows as dramatically as By The Hand, the danger is that procedures and policies grow willy-nilly and their original purpose gets lost in a fog of bureaucracy that with time gets only thicker. This fog can also put the brand mission into unfortunate shadow. If you sense this is the case in your company, the way around it is with periodic one-on-one contact with your staff to weed out their misunderstandings and to pull by the roots unnecessary bureaucratic pests. Donnita does this regularly. The process also turns up ways to improve performance and is one that shows how much you value staff input. It gives staff more stake in the brand's content and performance. As Yogi Berra once said, "You hear a lot just by listening." One-on-one findings can in turn be shared with all the players, which further shows your ability to listen and learn.

INNOVATION

We know that great brands never find comfort in standing still. By The Hand started with one location and is now in four. A charter school is also in the works, which will allow the brand to go further and more deeply with its mission. Blended learning will include the use of technology for personalized learning, allowing the kids to accelerate individually at their own pace.

The expression "no child left behind" truly comes to life under the shelter of this brand, and who knows how its mission and methods may spread to other American communities in the U.S. to break cycles of poverty and disadvantage through education. Certainly no patent exists to prevent it because no one can put a patent on doing the right thing. Social epidemics have started with less reason, and as Donnita would say, "this one little miracle in this one community is guided by the hand of God—a quite formidable sponsor!"

SEPTEMBER 11, 2001

Was there prophecy in By The Hand's beginning on the day that shook the world with terror? Donnita tells the story in her own words:

"There was great excitement and a certain nervousness for our small staff and the forty-two kids we started with. Then, when we all saw our TV screens light up with the horror of planes crashing into the World Trade Center, my phone blew up with phone calls wanting to know if we would open or tell everyone to stay home as recommended on the news. Everybody was worried that the Sears Tower here in Chicago would be another target.

But I decided that if the kids ever needed us, it would be on this day when they have more to fear than ever. At the time, Cabrini Green had a lot of high-rise apartment houses. It was easy for the kids to see themselves as targets, and I thought just having them with us so we could love them and reassure them would be the best course of action. I saw 9/11 as a metaphor for what goes on in Cabrini Green every day that the kids are exposed to fear and danger. It sounds a little presumptuous, and I would never describe myself in this way, but others have said we were a little like the firefighters running into the burning buildings to save victims while everybody else is running away from them—but that's how our neighborhoods are. We did open, and we are all glad we did. It turned out to be a great way to start the kids' experience with a safe haven in the face of terror."

Not many brands get this kind of dramatic opportunity to prove they are on the side of the angels, but many brands do intercede in the face of catastrophe. Walmart came to the rescue of victims of the Gulf hurricane with food and water by the truckload. Eveready came to the rescue with free batteries and cell power charges for cell phones. The Red Cross and the Salvation Army are two other nonprofits always standing by to do their bit. Organizations like Doctors Without Borders go beyond the call of duty to bring medical care to the world's most remote and needy people. We hear of individual acts of heroism performed by people in the media every day. It all makes being a member of the human race not seem such a bad club to be in after all.

There are many who think the profit motive is the only reason why brands exist. But as we have seen on the journey of this book, it is the brands that do care, that put a value on the lives and contributions of their workers and do what they can to improve the lives and experiences of their customers, that are most likely to survive and prosper. We have seen many exceptional examples. There are many more that would take another thousand pages to explore. But the conclusion is quite simple: Doing the right thing yields enormously positive consequences. The cost is low and the return is incredibly high. You only need to make two little changes—the way you think about your customers and the way you go about your business. Your employees will find meaning and motivation in their work. Customers will realize functional and emotional benefits that make them feel connected to your brand. In return, your brand will earn the irrational loyalty it needs to become truly trusted and successful. As we have seen in some of the best, most enlightened, most successful corporate cultures of our era, little things produce big returns.

A TRIBUTE TO HARRY

JUST WEEKS AFTER COMPLETING THE FIRST DRAFT OF THE manuscript for this book Harrison Yates, my dear friend and writing partner, passed away. Over the course of more than twenty years, Harry and I worked together in the advertising agency business and then collaborated on three books about building brands.

Harry was a highly lauded and awarded advertising copywriter and creative director. He worked closely with advertising greats David Ogilvy and Bill Bernbach on many famous campaigns including the legendary, industry-changing Volkswagen work. Harry created wonderful advertising to the very last, often joking that he was "the world's oldest working copywriter."

Harry was truly one of my most favorite people in the world and my favorite writer not only because he was just terrific at it but also because he could literally take piles of my ideas and notions and turn them into something readable and meaningful. Over the years, I came to look forward to notes or emails from Harry because his words often left me in stiches or made me stop to think more than once about what he had said. Harry's instinctive ability to cut to the chase and discern the most insightful thing was simply uncanny. Here in his own words is how he thought we should wrap up this book:

THE LAST WORD, I PROMISE

WRITING FOR ME IS A WAY OF THINKING IN THAT IT FORCES ME TO strive for clarity and consolidation in my thought process. You can't fake what you put on a blank page without it being obvious to yourself and others.

Ernest Hemingway said one should write drunk and edit sober. What he meant by the drunk bit, of course, is that you must let your thinking fly with no holds barred until you hit upon what you believe is the best, most involving way to make your hoped-for pearls of wisdom perfectly clear and hopefully involving.

As for editing sober, the cold light of day after your fingers have left the computer shows up all the sloppy thinking, poor use of particular words, slips in logic, poor syntax, and glaring inadequacies of intellect that force you to go back and start again. More than once in writing this book have I wondered why I submit myself to such compulsive torture. It can only mean in my case that I have a passionate interest in the subject matter. And indeed I do.

I hope you have felt Harry's passion in this book. I trust you have sensed not only his talent but his amazing joie de vivre, as well. It is sobering to know we will never again benefit from his words or enjoy his indomitable spirit beyond what has been written here. We will truly miss Harry's passion for life, his infectious humor, clear insights and inspiring words.

We will miss you Harry.

ACKNOWLEDGEMENTS

I LOVE THE ACKNOWLEDGEMENTS BECAUSE IT'S THE LAST THING I complete and it means the book is finally done. Believe me as long as it takes to live and suffer through bringing a book to life the words "it's done" are the best thing you can ever say.

It also means it is time to thank everyone who pushed, cajoled, nudged, contributed ideas and generally helped and encouraged the book to move forward in spite of the authors' misdirection, distractions, ceaseless attention deficit disorder and limited bandwidth.

Many on the team at Brandtrust frequently ask, "How's the book coming?" Though they may not always realize it, their terrific work on many of the world's best brands informs the stories in the book and their interest in the book inspires me to keep it moving along until it's finally finished.

In particular, Ed Jimenez created the beautiful book cover and text pages design. Valerie Penrose and Gillian Carter masterfully managed my schedule, the production milestones, and many of the marketing initiatives for the book. Thank you both for your amazing patience and commitment.

The three books that Harry and I completed together were lovingly read and critically edited by Harry's wonderful wife Monique. Like the others, this book is better because of Monique's time and talent.

Melissa Wilson and her Networlding team once again have been so helpful with the editing, publishing and promotional details of the book.

Several of the chapters were created directly from interviews graciously granted by Mike Bergman, Ben Brenton, Tom Feeney, Seth Goldman, Ginger Hardage, Bob Riney, Robert Willet and of course, my own, Donnita Travis. Thanks to all of you for your amazing work doing the little things that make a big difference in people's lives.

ABOUT DARYL TRAVIS

A TRUSTED ADVISOR TO MANY LEADING BRANDS, DARYL TRAVIS is a rare breed of author, thought leader and highly regarded consultant to many of the world's leading brands. His first book Emotional Branding pioneered the idea that brands are largely about feelings not facts.

As Founder and CEO of Brandtrust, his teams apply social and behavioral science to reveal deeper human truths that solve complex brand, innovation and customer experience challenges for many global brands.

He could be described as a professor, detective, psychologist and journalist all rolled into one. A colorful and engaging storyteller, Daryl writes and speaks frequently on the power of human truths to change everything including how you think about your customers and your business.

INDEX